What If I'm
~~Not~~ Enough?

Confronting the <u>Reflection</u>.
Releasing the <u>Fear</u>.
Owning the <u>Story</u>.

Teron Buford

CONTENTS

Gratitude

I 'LL KEEP THIS SHORT and sweet: my wife encouraged me to pick up writing as an outlet during a time when my mental health became so overwhelmed by the hurt and hardship occurring in the world around me that I began to fall headlong into a pit of grief and despair. I went down anxious rabbit hole after anxious rabbit hole until I landed on the conclusion that, since I couldn't control *everything* that accompanied the sensory and emotional overload we'd come to know as just another day in the life, then I couldn't control *anything* at all. In hindsight, you and I can see the fault in that logic but, in the moment, that was my reality.

I wrote this book as a form of therapy, and honestly, never expected anyone beyond a few close friends and family to read it. And now, with my words clutched tightly in hand, I can only assume one of two things about you, the reader:

1. You're a friend or family member consuming this to show love and support while also getting a quick peek behind the curtain of "What Makes Teron Tick," or

2. By picking this up, you've chosen to become a member of my team, and I, yours.

Either way, I'm grateful you're here. Thank you for listening to my truths and maybe learning from some of my mistakes and lessons along the way.

Love you, old and new family and friends.

Love you more, DeJurnett (Dee).

Setting the Scene

Grace Through Soul

THE DEAL

I F I'M BEING GENEROUS, I'd call myself an average reader, but to be honest, I'm way below that line. Reading has never come easy for me: it's slow, my comprehension is shaky, and sometimes I drift off mid-page, circling back and rereading the same paragraph several times for clarity, and still fall well short of understanding the content. I used to force my way through books to prove to myself that I might enjoy it given enough time and effort, but that was one of the worst things I could've possibly done– picking up literature that didn't fit my needs, realizing it *way* too late, quitting halfway through, and feeling like an abject failure. This only confirmed the narrative that I was "bad" at reading in the first place.

I won't do that to you. I'd never subject someone to the pain of slogging through material they can't connect with or force-feed items off my menu they can't stomach. So, here's the deal: in the following pages, I'm going to make five statements that sum up this book, its content and format. If none of them resonate, please set this piece down and find something better suited for you. But, if even *one* statement lands well, keep going. As the story and lessons mature, I'm confident you'll vibe with what I'm putting out into the world, feel a little less like the "lonely-only," or gain a perspective you didn't have before. And who knows, you might also fast-track your adventure into self-discovery, take permission to tend to your personal, physical, and mental health, or simply permit yourself to kindly reflect on who you are in this world while building the confidence to advance toward whoever it is you'd like to be.

Heads Up

While I want you to authentically engage with my story, it's more important that you do so with informed consent. This book touches on moments that were difficult for me to recount and may be triggering for you to read. Please take care to prioritize your personal, spiritual, and mental wellbeing. For transparency, I've included a list of challenging concepts I'll be referencing:

Addiction/Substance Abuse

Child Abuse

Domestic Violence/Abuse

Gang/Physical Violence

Grief and Death/Loss (including death of a child)

Mental Health

Sexual Abuse

Terminal Illness/Cancer

Premature Childbirth

Five Statements

1. Your Eyes. My Lens

I'M GOING TO BE straight with you— some parts of my story might sound shocking or unbelievable. As I said in the foreword, I only expected this book to be read by family, friends, and acquaintances. So while not all of this is news to them, to those who don't yet know me there are some hard truths, challenging stories, triggering moments, and traumatic experiences incoming. I'll flesh out the entire story as we go along, sometimes jumping back and forth along my timeline, but for now, here's the short version:

I was born in Chicago, IL, two months prematurely after my father punched my mother while she was pregnant. I came into this world weighing barely four or five pounds, and severely addicted to cocaine because of a debilitating habit my mother couldn't kick even after finding out she was carrying me. I grew up surrounded by gangs, drugs, violence, grandmotherly love, and cousin relationships that were so tight that they were more akin to siblings than anything else. At one point, there were sixteen of us in a two-bedroom apartment on the West Side, yet somehow it never felt crowded. We rarely got attached to any living situation, however, because we could set our watches to the annual traditions of missed rent, eviction notices, and frantic scrambles to find another place to stay. This led to me attending a total of eight different elementary and high schools over the course of thirteen years. My grandmother was the glue that held our unit together— when she died, our family barreled head-first into a downward spiral that resulted in me couch-hopping for a couple of months. Eventually I ended up spending about a year in a homeless shelter with my mother and two younger sisters (Tameka and Tachena) in a new and foreign state six hours north of the only place I'd ever known as home.

But this book isn't a trauma-brag; I'm giving you the facts so you can see the whole picture. Today, I live in a stable home with my beautiful, strong, and brilliant wife, our family cat, and two semi-lovely kids (no shade– the parents out there know what I mean). I've got a good career, rock ugly sweaters during the holidays, drive a basic three-row SUV, sweeten my baked goods with monk fruit, prefer avocados as my healthy source of fat, and occasionally find myself sipping on a kombucha after a long day of work. Fifteen-year-old Teron would be staring at me, shaking his head and asking, "Bro... what *happened*?" If you stay tuned, that question will be answered for him (and you) over the course of these pages.

2. Agreements

Before I facilitate any deep discussions—or as folks like to call them, trainings (ugh, we train pets; we *educate* people)—I start with grounding agreements. The first is **Courage**, which calls us to be bold and honest in our interactions. Next is **Trust**, enabling us to instill confidence and integrity in ourselves and others, especially during moments of vulnerability. **Grace** is the third commitment, it provides us with the freedom to extend and receive patience and empathy. **Active Listening** necessarily follows, it grants us the ability to practice engagement for understanding, not rebuttal or argumentation. Next, I ask that we commit to **Growth and Development**, which requires that we meaningfully *do* something with the learnings, as opposed to simply sitting on the content, allowing it to waste away. Finally, we commit to **Radical Candor**, or the promise to hold ourselves and others accountable for the betterment of all.

As I lean into these agreements, I invite you to do the same. Reflect with courage. Trust yourself as the foremost expert on your story. Give yourself the grace you give others. Listen without judgment. And when the lessons hit, don't just nod, act. Ask yourself, "So what?" What will you start, stop, or continue in service of your growth?

3. Imperfections

Imposter syndrome has often convinced me my best wasn't good enough. That perfection was the goal, and anything short of that meant failure. It didn't help that I grew up hearing motivational phrases like "practice makes perfect" or seeing folks flex their perfectionism like a badge of honor all while ignoring how toxic both ideologies can be (and usually are) if left unchecked. It wasn't until I was much older that I discovered how the pursuit of "perfect" pushes us to become obsessed with every detail, and many times, paralyzed by the fear of judgment when we fall short of that impossible standard.

It took my then-six-year-old daughter to call it out one day after gymnastics practice, correcting what I intended as encouragement without skipping a beat: "Dad, practice doesn't make perfect; it makes *progress*." I'll tell you what— moments like those knock me flat on my butt. Equal parts proud and humbled, both courtesy of a person who couldn't yet tie her shoes, let alone spell the word chastise. Don't get me wrong, grinding and putting in sweat equity are important and there *are* people who *do* need to work twice as hard for half the recognition. That's real. But being hard on ourselves to the point of breakdown isn't noble. It's destructive.

4. Hard Work

"Pull yourself up by your bootstraps."

"Keep your head down and work hard."

"Hard work outshines talent when talent doesn't work hard."

We've all heard these proverbs before, and while they aren't entirely wrong, they're woefully incomplete. Take my childhood friend, LaTrell, for example. Even as kids, I knew he had me beat at every turn. He was smarter, more talented, and more driven than I'd ever been. He had dreams bigger than mine, the grit to match, and unfortunately, a fate that contradicted his potential. While I sit before you today with the luxury of writing for leisure, LaTrell was murdered four days before his seventeenth birthday after an argument at a house party.

No matter how driven he was or how hard he worked, there was one thing I had that he didn't. Some people call it luck or fortune or blessings—whatever. But we all know someone who ended up in the right (or wrong) place at the right (or wrong) time, and it changed everything. Those are the breaks, and the sooner I accepted that truth, the sooner I could make peace with surviving in a world absent LaTrell while also imparting a bit of grace into my life when circumstances pelted me with rocks at every chance imaginable. We can't always control when or to what degree life knocks us down, but if the blow doesn't prove fatal, what's more important is that we find the vulnerable courage to ask for help as we attempt to stand back up.

Side note: ever *actually* tried pulling yourself up by your boot-straps? Give it a shot. Lay on the ground, grab that little loopy thing on the back of your shoe, and then try to stand. Physically impossible and potentially the dumbest saying to ever be uttered.[1]

5. Bad Decisions, Fortunate Breaks, and Terrible Dad Jokes

My mom always saw me as an angel. Maybe it was guilt or a little bit of denial, but even when I got caught red-handed in mischief, she tended to let it slide or believe whatever nonsensical excuse I choked out in the moment. Given my whimsical birth story and the narrative that lies ahead, it should come as no surprise that she and I had a complicated and challenging relationship over the years. But when I became a dad myself, something shifted between us, almost cosmetically fixing things overnight. We never really dealt with our trauma, but we got really good at tiptoeing around it like the vicious neighborhood dog who could slip through the cracks in its poorly-constructed and flimsy fence. Always keeping an eye on it and praying it wouldn't attack.

One day, feeling bold and honest, I told her everything, and I mean *everything*, about my childhood antics, hoping my transparency would strengthen our bond, take our relationship to the next level and maybe—oh, I don't know—inspire her to own up to some of her own misdeeds, giving us the opportunity to finally address, reconcile, and move beyond them. Yeah... that was dumb. This book is full of bad decisions I made, fortunate breaks I caught, and lessons I learned the hard way. I'll try to spell some out, but sometimes you'll have to read between the lines and connect a few dots as you put it all together for yourself. I promise, though, if you stick with it (and me), it'll be worth it in the long run.

Also, fair warning: I process life through metaphors, similes, analogies, and make heavy use of sarcasm and hyperbolic jokes to ease tension or lighten the room. And yes, occasionally that means a bad dad joke or two will slip in. Sometimes they'll be more subtle while others will be more apparent (Get it? Apparent. A Parent. Because...dad...? Yeah, I'm sorry. That was rough).

---

1. Ironically, this saying gained popularity as a sarcastic reference to an impossible task, but over time, became a motto of self-reliance.

Fault—Responsibility—Fault

I F YOU'VE MADE IT this far, welcome. Just one more thing I need to introduce, a concept I call *fault-responsibility-fault*. Here's how it works—you're not at fault for the circumstances you're unwilfully tossed into, but once you become aware of the problems and have the wherewithal to impact them, it becomes your *responsibility* to act. If you choose to neglect that obligation and harm, pain, or damage subsequently follows, it's hard not to count that as *your* fault.

My wife and I bought our first house in 2012. It wasn't much, but it was ours, and after signing the approximate 12 million pages of paperwork, we were hit with a rush of self-fulfillment and accomplishment. Standing strong since 1927 and complete with a structurally sound foundation and heaping helping of tightly packed and mostly concealed asbestos, what could possibly go wrong? One day, I noticed a puddle in the kitchen but figured it was just a spill. Paid it no mind. Next day, same spot. Only now there was a noticeable drip coming from the ceiling that I lazily patched, thinking that'd do the trick. To the surprise of no one who's ever worked in construction or has a basic understanding of how water functions, what followed was a full-blown collapse that required a complete ceiling and roof replacement.

While my carpenter stepdad helped me DIY it, the real lesson was in the framing (construction pun, sorry) of the scenario. The leak wasn't my **fault**. That was an issue that likely existed before we moved in but, since we hadn't had any rain that fall, we wouldn't have recognized it until the spring after the snow started to melt. The **responsibility** to fix it *was* mine, but since I went with the band-aid approach instead of addressing the problem at its root, the resulting damage that occurred *was* all my **fault**. That's it. Fault → Responsibility → Fault. Take note, you'll see it pop up a few more times.

Fear

"Hey, Teron. The title of the book references fear, but you haven't touched on it yet. What's the deal?" Good question. Fear, both loud and quiet, threads itself through this entire book. How we let it define and limit us, or how we use it as an excuse to avoid the hard things we know, deep down, we *should* do. It gives us a convenient off-ramp when something feels too daunting, unfamiliar, or just plain uncomfortable. Fear feeds our political divides, helps us rationalize hate and distrust, gives us cover to dehumanize what we don't understand, sparks wars, and has even taken lives. F-E-A-R: four little letters forming one enormous, complex force.

But let me be clear: fear isn't always the villain, it serves a purpose. Without it, my one hundred-times-great-grandfather (shoutout to Grandpa Grunk) might've tried to pet a saber-toothed tiger, strolled carelessly into a pitch-black forest at night, or casually walked off a cliff, and had he done any of those things, I probably wouldn't be here today. From an evolutionary standpoint, we *need* fear. And while I'm not a neuroscientist (so please, brain experts, don't come for me), I'm pretty sure fear is processed in the area nestled near the base of your skull where it meets the spine, known as the amygdala.

It handles our fight, flight, freeze, and fawn responses. When a stimulus enters the brain, it tends to pass through that region first, like a filter. If it doesn't set off any alarms, it slips through. But if even the slightest trace of danger is detected, the amygdala flares and readies us to hide under a table, bolt for the nearest exit or throw hands. Fear keeps us alert and alive, but it was never meant to act alone.

Like most powerful forces, fear needs checks and balances. Enter logic and reason. These two MVPs, when called upon, help us interrogate, understand, and sometimes even dissolve fear. That's why most adults no longer believe there are monsters under their beds or why I'm no longer afraid to say "Candyman" in the mirror five times (millennials and Gen Xers, you know what I mean).

Logic and reason live in the prefrontal cortex—way up front in your brain, which matters because to move fear from the amygdala to the prefrontal cortex, the thought has to travel a *long* way. And here's the kicker you might've missed earlier: while fear is sometimes learned but mostly instinctual, logic and reason must be *invited*. Fear shows up unannounced, but logic and reason have to be called in. That means you can naturally coast through life letting fear dictate your decisions without even trying. It *wants* to take the wheel. But logic and reason? They require effort, intention, and when you're afraid, that effort can feel unnatural.

Key word: feel.

My way of moving fear from the base of my brain to the top doesn't involve rocket science or a PhD. It just takes a little time, honesty, and vulnerability. When I'm feeling afraid, but know I'm not in any immediate danger, I ask myself a few small but mighty questions:

1. **Where is this fear coming from? What's it rooted in? Why?**

2. **Am I afraid because there's an actual threat or just because something is different, new, or uncomfortable? Why?**

3. **If I let my guard down, what's (reasonably) the worst that could happen? Why?**

Now, I'm not suggesting you pause and reflect in every fearful moment. Let's not be ridiculous. If I hear a loud bang or see people sprinting away from the source of an alarming sound, I'm not standing around wondering, *"Hmm, what's the origin of my concern here?"* No. I'm dashing out of there, too. We'll debrief about what we were running from whenever we get to wherever we're going. But when the threat isn't immediate or life-threatening? That's when I try to pause, sit with the emotion, hold it up to the light, and ask those questions. Because uninterrogated fear breeds unnecessary anxiety and stress.

This book is full of moments where fear showed up in my life. Sometimes I faced it. Other times, it punked me. I'm not perfect, but I *am* inviting you to take a look at your fear, ask yourself the questions, and investigate if it's standing in your way for no good reason.

A'ight. Let's get to it.

Humble Beginnings

Grace Through Soul

HUMBLE BEGINNINGS

I N FULL DISCLOSURE, I'M going to be talking about memories of my mother and father, which will include graphic accounts of domestic abuse. I debated how much detail to include, torn between the shame of my memories and the risk of traumatizing anyone reading along. And while I wish I could say those were my only reasons, or that you'd see me as thoughtful or noble for considering them, I can't.

In the introduction I referenced courage, and if I'm keeping it real, I'm not sure I have the strength to tell you—or myself—just how afraid I am to write authentically about my mom and dad. For as long as I draw breath, I'll believe the old adage my Granny used to say to me as a boy: "Baby, let me tell you something right now. When it comes to dealing with people and their memories, there are always three sides to the story: yours, theirs, and the truth." Bear with me as I try to find the honesty, boldness, and conviction to pry open the vaults that have locked away pains so deep I only visit them when absolutely necessary. This is my truth.

You know how we tend to over-remember the bad and gloss over the good? I'm afraid that's what this account will do. I worry you'll read what I lived through and form a judgment of my parents based only on what I recall—that you'll see my mother as nothing more than a crackhead chasing her next high or my father as an abusive monster who used his hands as weapons. But more than anything, I fear I won't be able to show you how deeply I believe my parents loved me.

When my mother wasn't in desperate need of a fix or behind bars, I like to think she was doing her best to nurture and care for us. And sometimes I can bring myself to understand that my dad didn't hurt us out of hatred, but because, in his own way, that's how he thought love and discipline worked. Maybe when we disappointed him or fell short of his expectations, he believed the best way to correct us was through force. And maybe I'm just making excuses. I don't know. But I'll tell you this: for all the hardship, somewhere deep inside both of them was a kind of love. It didn't always feel like it, but I believe it was there.

And if I'm keeping it *really* real, I'm terrified that the next time you see me, whatever respect or admiration you once held will dissolve into pity, sympathy, or contemplations akin to, "Oh, you poor baby," or, "Wow, he's been through so much." That's not the aim of this book. So, I'm going to try to lean on a couple of the concepts I referenced in the intro, mainly the one about moving fear into the rational part of the brain, as I talk about the hard things.

A Child Is Born

March 23. By all accounts, that should've been my arrival date—a spring birthday with halfway decent weather and a shot at overlapping with spring break. Man, that would've been sweet. I could've pretended school was out just for me, taking the full seven days to celebrate without worrying about homework, projects, bedtimes, or alarm clocks. But that wasn't in the cards. Instead, I was born two months early, thanks to a toxic manifestation of love that too often goes unaddressed. I don't know all the details, but I know my parents had gotten into a fight, and a punch from my father sent my mother into premature labor.

I came into the world weighing between four and five pounds, and since my mother couldn't kick her drug habit—not even while pregnant—I was born severely addicted to cocaine. My lungs were underdeveloped, which led to me having an asthma attack, losing another pound or two, and spending several weeks in the neonatal intensive care unit while the medical staff worked to bring me up to an acceptable level of health.

You might be wondering, "How could the doctors and social workers let him go home with his family after all that?" You've got to understand– my birth story wasn't unique, special, or even new. Where I'm from, tons of babies came into the world under similar circumstances, and I imagine the Department of Children and Family Services was already stretched thin, overworked, and overwhelmed by more urgent cases to be that worried about mine. Such is life.

Eyes On The Road

One of my earliest and most cherished memories of my father is from when he pretended to teach me how to drive, and in his own way, how to win the favor of a potential partner. I was maybe six or seven years old the first time he sat me on his lap in the driver's seat as he worked the gas and brake pedals while I steered us down the street. Now, before you go all "Oh my gosh, how could he!?" on me, relax. He was probably only doing ten miles per hour, kept his hand on the lower part of the steering wheel, and made plenty of course corrections anytime I veered too far in either direction. We stuck to side streets with one-way traffic and avoided areas full of kids running around (I think. I hope).

For this next part, do yourself a favor and read it in your best Australian accent. Pretend you're on a safari, documenting and narrating everything you see:

The father understands it is vital to teach his son how to court a suitable partner if he is to ever mate and reign over his territory. As they move about the area, the mature male spots a potential female on which to demonstrate the most effective technique. The father signals the son to watch closely as he honks the car horn twice (any fewer wouldn't attract enough attention, but any more might seem desperate). The adult male leans toward the passenger-side window, winks his right eye, and nods downward as if to say, "Hey, baby, you want a ride?" He then motions to the boy; it's HIS turn to try. They drive a few hundred feet up and spot the next woman to grace with their presence. The boy presses the horn twice, but he's not strong or coordinated enough, so what should sound like two sharp honks ends up being one long and one short, spaced out just far enough to sound awkward. He tries to wink but realizes he's never done it before, so instead, he rapidly blinks at her five or six times through the window. He attempts a nod but ends up doing more of a ceremonial bow.

Ultimately, instead of "Hey baby, you need a ride?" it comes off more like, "Hello, fair maiden, my eyes are broken and require immediate medical attention. Can you assist?"

My relationship with my father was complicated. How could the man who violently expedited my arrival into the world and refused to put his name on my birth certificate be the same person who later took pride in watching me become a miniature version of himself? I can still hear his lessons like he whispered them to me yesterday— "Always take care of your mother and sisters," "Don't start a fight but always finish them," "Work hard in school," "Never hit a woman,"— yeah, that last one was a hard pill to swallow, especially after seeing him beat the hell out of my mother on more than one occasion, with the worst of them taking place at our little apartment on the edge of Oak Park and Chicago.

User Error

I couldn't have been more than five years old when my dad started teaching me his version of gun safety. "Guns are not a toy. Guns are tools for self-defense. Never pull out a gun if you don't plan to use it. Never point a gun at something you don't want to kill." Solid advice between kindergarten homework and after-school cartoons, but I digress. I should note, my dad was a "boss"—a high-ranking gang member who made a lot of money selling drugs and enforcing street justice with cold, militaristic precision. He liked things done a certain way and lived by a code that could only respond to treachery or disloyalty with swift, severe force. You'd think a man with such standards wouldn't partner with a woman whose addiction ran so deep she'd do just about anything for her next high, but here we are.

One day my mother was jonesing, which wasn't really anything new. But this time, instead of targeting one of her usual safe marks, she took a few hundred dollars from my dad's roll. When he found out, there was hell to pay. What I witnessed that day was the most violent assault I've ever seen in my entire life. He beat my mother with what looked like all his strength. Belts. Slaps. Fists. Body slams. It went on for what felt like hours. You know those wooden paddle boards that fraternities hang on their walls? My dad had one that he'd drilled holes into to reduce wind resistance and increase impact. It was meant for intruders foolish enough to break into our apartment, but that day, it became a weapon against a woman he claimed to love.

I remember watching in a kind of paralyzed disbelief as he ripped the paddle off the wall and swung it toward my mother's face with full-force, tee-off strength. Had it connected, there's no question—she would have died. Call it luck, grace, divine intervention, or whatever you'd like, but, mid-swing, the board snapped in half. I don't know if the holes weakened it, if it clipped the door frame, or if a heavenly being reached down and said, "Enough," but the fatal blow never landed. And there I was. Right there. Watching everything. Screaming, crying, and begging him to pull back.

"Please! Stop! Leave her alone!"

My mother, bloodied and crying, screamed, "Call the police, Teron!" I ran to the landline, trembling, dialing, until my father's voice cut through the air like a blade.

"You better put that motherf***ing phone down right now,

boy!"

"Teron, PLEASE!" my mother yelled again.

"SIT. YOUR. ASS. DOWN!" he shouted.

They went back and forth like that—her pleading, him bark-ing—until I couldn't take it anymore. I collapsed on the floor, curled up into the fetal position, and rocked back and forth while cradling the phone like a child I had failed to protect. Inconsolable. Five years old.

Eventually the beating stopped, my father went to bed, my mother refused to go to the hospital, and I stayed awake, re-playing every moment of what had just happened. And this is where things get hazy because I don't remember anything after I retreated to my bedroom. All I have are the sworn accounts of my mother, father, and eldest sister, each of them telling me the same story, years apart, with no deviations. According to them, my father woke up around 11:00 p.m. to a strange sound above his head—a rhythmic, mechanical clicking. He rolled over, wiped his eyes, and stared down the barrel of a nine-millimeter pistol. Behind the gun stood a small boy struggling to hold the five-pound weapon steady: me.

The clicking? That was me pulling the trigger over and over, trying to fire but, since I'd failed to properly load the magazine, I was unsuccessful in chambering a round. Click. Click. Click. Nothing. You want to talk about lucky breaks? If I'd been just a little stronger or a better listener during his "lessons," I might be in a very different place today. Ironically, I was following the training he gave me, trying to protect my mother and eliminate the threat to my family. I don't remember how he responded to my toddler-sized version of attempted murder masquerading as guardianship, but if it's true that leopards don't change their spots, it probably wasn't mercifully.

Like most abusive relationships, the makeup and honeymoon phases were euphoric. I remember trips to toy stores, motorized cars, toy airplanes, bikes—you name it. When my dad was around, we "had it like that." For all the violence and fear, there was also financial stability. That's the dilemma we faced. A present father with money and the occasional violent outburst, or a single-parent household with greater safety but constant financial struggle. We navigated that impossible math as my father rotated in and out of prison. When he was gone, money got tight, leaving us with not enough to cover everything. Some months we lived without electricity, a working phone, or hot water. Rent was hit-or-miss and once our landlords had enough of our excuses, eviction notices became a seasonal occurrence. Five different elementary schools. Three different high schools. To this day, I have no idea how I met the standards to move from one grade to the next.

Protecting The Homefront

I got my first job at the ripe old age of eight. We were living with my grandmother at the time in her two-bedroom apartment on the west side of Chicago. On any given day, there were no fewer than twelve—and sometimes as many as sixteen or eighteen—people living there. Beatrice Buford. Grandma Beatrice. Sweet Bea. Granny. The closest thing to a saint I've ever known. That woman believed in me so deeply, I can't help but wonder where I'd be without her. That was my lady, and I was her baby.

No two ways about it. She was everything. She'll get more than just a paragraph, believe that. But I had to mention her here because, even though she loved me, lifted me, and made me feel seen, I still managed to let her down. She didn't know it, but I did.

While it didn't come with an I-9, W-2, benefits, or vacation days, my first job suited me well. Every now and then, I worked "security" on my block. For those who might be unaware, gangs and criminal organizations operate a lot like brick-and-mortar businesses. There's a hierarchy of respect and decision-making, market analysis, supply chain management, product placement, customer relations, and accounting. Sure, the HR department isn't exactly equipped with peer mediators and accepting coupons is generally frowned upon, but outside of that, these organizations functioned just like your local supermarket (you know, if your supermarket sold cocaine, armed its employees with semiautomatics, and literally eliminated the competition).

Jokes aside, most of the drug dealers I knew were some of the most decisive, business-savvy, and hard-working people around. They could take a brick of product, chop it up just right, and turn a profit for themselves, their suppliers, and the street-level "vendors" doing the day-to-day sales. The biggest difference between a Fortune-500 CEO and a hood boss? One is admired for their insatiable appetite to dominate the market, while the other gets labeled immoral or criminal by the same systems that created their social, political, and economic oppression. But that's a conversation for another day.

Like any good company, someone had to be at the door—someone to keep watch, alert the team when danger was near, and tell them when to pause operations. Someone to spot the cops and let everyone know it was time to course-correct. That's where I came in. For a few bucks a day, I'd sit on Granny's porch and call out a code word that would echo down the block from one lookout to the next. That warning let the dealers know it was time to shut everything down until the danger had passed. I'd shout, "LIGHTS OUT," which began the ripple of parroted alerts down the block. Once the police were gone, we'd give the all-clear for business practices to resume.

One day, an undercover squad car slipped through the cracks, which resulted in the arrest of Stacy, a high-ranking member of the local criminal organization. Getting him was a huge win for Chicago PD, and unfortunately it happened on my watch. I witnessed the entire interaction as they pulled him out of the car, slammed him against the hood, rifled through his pockets, and shoved him into the backseat. My lapse in vigilance would've been met with intense punishment had it not been for what happened next.

Two of the officers grabbed Stacy's keys and started eyeing his vehicle like they had a plan. Stacy's car—a dark green, two-door old-school whip with pitch-black tinted windows and a bumpin' sound system—was unmistakable. Everybody knew it, and if seen rolling down the block, no one would think twice, continuing with business as usual, which is exactly what the cops were counting on. They'd pulled off a modern-day Trojan Horse, figuring they could scoop up a few more dealers by cruising around in Stacy's car and catching folks with their guards down. Genius, in a way, if you ignore the blatant abuse of authority. But they hadn't accounted for one key detail: me.

Yeah, I'd messed up and failed to call out the initial warning, but I wasn't about to let more people get picked up on my shift. I rushed to some of the "middle managers," told them what I'd seen, and they passed the message down the line. The system worked, no other arrests were made that day, and thanks to a little Paul Revere-style alerting, I dodged what could've been some serious consequences.

Just Get Home

My mother was one of those sales associates. She sold drugs daily, partly to feed her addiction, partly to put food on the table. I won't get into the dangers of having someone addicted to cupcakes working in a bakery, but I bet you can piece that one together. My greatest failure as a security worker came the day I missed a *lights out* call, which led to my mother's arrest across the street from Granny's apartment. I stood there, frozen, along with my sisters and what felt like every cousin we had, watching helplessly as they cuffed and patted her down. We sobbed bitterly while my mother turned back to plead with someone—anyone—to get us inside.

"Go in the house," she begged. "Please, just go inside."

The officer barked, "Stand still! Look forward!"

But she didn't. She couldn't. She saw the fear in our eyes, the trauma settling in behind our tears, and did what any parent would do. She turned her head again.

"Please, somebody take them inside." This time, the officer lost it. He placed a hand on the back of her head and slammed her face into the hood of the car.

"LOOK. FORWARD." Our cries intensified at the sight. My mother turned once more, blood now streaming down her face, to beg us again to go inside. I ran—into the apartment, into the only place that felt safe—and did the exact thing every child had been taught to do when someone they love is being hurt.

"9-1-1, what's your emergency?"

"Help! Help," I begged, "the police are beating up my mom!" Seeing no other option, I called the cops... on the cops. I'll give you one guess whether a second squad car ever came to investigate.

Reality set in as I began to accept the fact that I likely wouldn't see my mother again for a few years without several inches of glass between us, but to everyone's surprise, that wasn't the case. Twenty minutes after the officers shoved my mother into the squad car, she inexplicably walked through Granny's front door. Her face swollen, shirt bloodied, and it was evident that someone had tried to clean her up. Confused, we asked why—how—she was back.

"They just let me go," she said.

Being eight years old, I believed her. Maybe the officers took pity. Maybe they saw us crying and had a change of heart. Maybe the one who slammed her head into the car realized he'd gone too far. I didn't know. I didn't care. I just knew I had my mom back. It wasn't until later in life that I learned the truth: in exchange for her freedom, she had to perform unspeakable acts on both officers in an alley a few blocks away.

Lessons Learned Part 1

D OES A FISH KNOW that it's in water? Probably not, right? It's just part of its existence—so mundane, so constant, it doesn't even notice. But does a fish know when it's *not* in water? Absolutely. It flops and gasps, desperate to return to its familiar depths or falls victim to an environment that can't sustain it. That was me. I had no idea my early years were abnormal until I was presented with something different. I accepted my reality because that's all I knew. You sleep on the floor on New Year's Day or whenever the professional basketball team wins a championship because the neighborhood celebrates by firing guns into the sky, and you've learned that what goes up must eventually come down. You come to terms with the fact that people die every day from gang violence or drug use, and that not much can be done about it. You know that if mom cooks a pot of spaghetti on Sunday, it means you'll be eating spaghetti for every meal until it's gone. Syrup sandwiches become a favorite treat. And if you're really lucky, you might find a quarter or two for penny candy at the corner store. People get evicted. The lights, gas, and water get shut off when the bills aren't paid. You sleep six to a bed, head-to-feet, and assume everyone is doing the best they can because that's all you've got to go on.

I had a college professor once challenge me with something that didn't make sense at the time but eventually clicked. "Teron," he said, "absent severe mental illness, everyone desires good. Enslavers. Hitler. You name it. They all believed in their version of 'good' and used that to justify how they got from A to Z." Now, I don't buy into that entirely, but I get the gist. The gang members in my community probably yearned for camaraderie and protection—desired good for self. The drug dealers were seeking financial stability and a way to provide—desired good for self. The users were chasing a momentary escape from a harsh, unrelenting reality—desired good for self. My dad... desired good for self?

If there's one thing I've come to believe, it's the importance of examining the root causes of perceived bad behavior. If it's true that people only crave good—and again, I'm not saying it is—then there has to be something deeper beneath the surface. Some rationale. Some distorted sense of purpose that justifies the pain they cause. Don't misunderstand me: knowing someone's motives doesn't absolve them from the consequences of their actions or the hurt they've caused, but it *can* shine a light on their humanity and what might be broken, lost, or learned.

Some of y'all might disagree with that. Call me naïve. Say I'm too forgiving. Truth be told, I think I disagree with it a little, too. But if I'm forced to believe that the symptoms of hardship, hatred, and evil exist without any treatment plan—without any possibility of healing or hope—I don't know if I could take it. So, I'm urging you (and myself) to hold on to that ounce of optimism buried deep in our hearts. The part that still wonders if, just maybe, a leopard *can* change its spots.

Man… life is complicated.

Cringe Year Chronicles

Grace Through Soul

CRINGE YEAR CHRONICLES

Y EARS TEN THROUGH SEVENTEEN were all about movement and agility. Sometimes metaphorically, but often literally. Up until then we never stayed in an apartment for more than maybe a year. Eighteen months, tops. By the time I made it to fifth grade, I'd already attended four different elementary schools and had no reason to believe that kind of instability was going to level out anytime soon. For anyone wondering how the math worked out: I was enrolled at School A for kindergarten and the first half of first grade, School B for the second half of first grade and all of second, School C for third, and wrapped up fourth grade at School D.

I'm intentionally leaving out the schools' names for two reasons. 1. if, by some stretch of the imagination, this book ever sees the light of day, I don't want to bring any undue negative attention their way. 2. I didn't have great experiences and don't want to put any of them on blast. Like School C, where the teachers and administrators used corporal punishment as a corrective tool for what they deemed to be disobedience or misbehavior. Dead serious, they would legitimately and severely hit the students almost daily, without hesitation. The gym teacher, as an example, would often take a jump rope and whip us across our arms if we didn't follow his exact instructions. Talking while he was? Wack! Not standing in line? Pop! Engaging in a little horseplay? Thump!

At one point, my mom had to go up to the school and threaten my third-grade teacher with bodily harm after I told her about an incident that happened just a day earlier. The class had been a little rowdy that morning so— let's call her Ms Johnson— ordered us to have silent lunch. She'd warned that if anyone made so much as a peep during the punishment, we'd be in even deeper trouble. I'll give you one guess who couldn't keep his mouth shut. In holding to her word, Ms. Johnson called me and a few others to the front of the class and slapped us across our faces. In truth, most wouldn't even classify it as a slap because it lacked any real force. It wasn't hard or painful and was meant to be more punitive and embarrassing than anything, but that's not how I sold it to my mother.

"Momma! Ms. Johnson slapped me today! In front of the whole class!"

That was all she needed to hear. The next morning she went straight to Ms. Johnson's classroom and told her off. While I wasn't in the room when it happened, my imagination led me to believe she said something like—"...and if you ever put your hands on my son again, I'ma knock your teeth so far down your throat you're gonna need to brush 'em up your ass!"— I don't know. Sounds like something she'd say. I'll tell you what, Ms. Johnson never touched me again.

School D was a much better experience for me, but I couldn't really hold up my academic or attendance ends of the bargain. In fourth grade, we got evicted. Twice, I think, as my mother and father were in and out of jail for selling drugs. That left me with my eldest and two younger sisters, a bunch of cousins, and... you guessed it, Granny. But by the time we settled in with her I'd already missed too many days of school, which left the administrators with no choice but to hold me back to repeat the fourth grade. But by the time they'd made that decision, my mother had gotten out of jail and wasn't having it. That summer she transferred me to School E.

THOMAS CHALMERS ELEMENTARY SCHOOL

I'M BREAKING MY RULE and calling this one out by name! It's by far the school I most identify with when I think about my life in Chicago. I attended from fifth through eighth grade when I experienced true housing stability for the first time in my life, though we had to do some shady things to hold on to it (if you ever need to learn how to steal cable TV in 1998, come holla at me).

Chalmers was an Afro-centric school, which meant it focused on the contributions that Black Americans made to the fabric of our society and worked hard to make sure we felt pride in our skin. That was important for me because up until that point, I'd mostly seen Black folks poorly portrayed in movies and on TV, but Chalmers came along and changed all that. This school is the reason I could recite "Lift Ev'ry Voice and Sing" before I knew "The Star-Spangled Banner." I still remember the poem we said aloud daily, "Be the Best of Whatever You Are" by Douglas Malloch (do yourself a favor and look it up). But the most memorable and important feature of Chalmers was the teachers. Quite a few left lasting impressions on me, and if you don't mind, I'd like to give them their flowers (with names changed to protect their privacy).

Smart? Who? Me?

First and foremost, there was Ms. Kizzy. If you're a millennial who attended Chalmers, you already know exactly who I'm talking about. Ms. Kizzy was that cool, auntie-esque teacher who could move effortlessly between dropping knowledge and showing you just how much she loved the work and her students. She brought warmth, presence, and intention into every lesson, making it virtually impossible not to be drawn to her. She made learning feel like play but never compromised the value of what she was teaching. Whether it was her clever use of math games like "Buzz" and "24," or the way she incentivized participation with her (now legendary) candy bowl, Ms. Kizzy knew how to tap into what motivated each of us. I think she saw how competitive we were and found a way to repurpose it for her and our betterment, teaching us that we could all be winners in our own right if we were willing to occasionally apply ourselves.

But Ms. Kizzy's real magic wasn't in her lesson plans or classroom management; it was in how she saw us. How she saw me. Until then I didn't have a strong sense of who I could be, never viewing myself as smart or capable of doing much of anything that mattered, but Ms. Kizzy came along and changed all that. She was the first teacher to tell me flat-out that I was intelligent. That I could grow up to be anything I wanted. And here's the thing— because she had built such a deep rapport with the class, earned our trust, and captivated our attention—

when she said it, I believed her. That was all it took. That one moment planted a seed that led to me aspiring to grow up and be somebody simply because she said so. That kind of belief, unconditional and unshakable, stayed with me. Still does. Love you, Ms. Kizzy.

I rode that wave of assurance straight into middle school. At Chalmers, sixth through eighth graders moved over to the "Upper Side" of the building, which meant a shift in structure and no more single-teacher classrooms. Instead, we switched from class to class, just like high school. That might seem ordinary to most, but for me, it was a brand-new rhythm that I welcomed with open arms. My sixth-grade homeroom teacher was none other than Mr. Jazzner. He was the very first male teacher I'd ever had, and let me tell you, he didn't pull his punches. Mr. Jazzner didn't just teach, he challenged. He had a knack for spotting potential and calling it out without apology. Early in our interactions he identified me as "gifted," and from then on, held me to that standard. There was no skating by on charm or excuses. If I gave subpar effort, he'd call it out—not to shame, but to remind me of who I was becoming. That mattered.

He taught me that pride in your work isn't just about grades, it's about character, and when I inevitably slipped up (because hormones and hallway scuffles happen), Mr. Jazzner didn't just discipline, he guided. When I got into a fight with a classmate, instead of pursuing suspension he sat us down—two angry, awkward preteens—and helped us talk through our differences. He gave us tools, language, and a space to process the emotions we barely understood ourselves. That kind of conflict resolution was unheard of at the time. Normally, a fight meant automatic suspension, no questions asked. But Mr. Jazzner chose a different path. He modeled the kind of patient, restorative leadership I hadn't seen before. Now, as an adult, I realize just how much it's shaped the way I approach conflict, difficult discussions, and interpersonal relationships. Love you, Mr. Jazzner.

Then came Mr. Moore, my seventh-grade homeroom teacher and the first White male educator I'd ever had. And listen, I need you to believe me when I say that Mr. Moore was one of the coolest dudes I've ever met in my life. It's going to sound corny, but this guy wore short-sleeve tees under patterned sweater vests with the crispiest creased jeans you've ever seen. My man was fresh to death and I was here for every bit of it. But Mr. Moore's impact went so far beyond his wardrobe; he also embodied thoughtfulness, intellect, and presence in a way that felt cinematic. Like, it was straight out of a '90s movie. You know the one where the White teacher shows up at an all-Black school and changes everything? Except this wasn't a savior story. Mr. Moore never centered himself, he simply met us where we were, saw who we could be, and walked alongside us on the journey.

One of the most powerful tools he introduced us to was chess. Yeah, chess. He said it was about learning to think several steps ahead, anticipating your opponent's next move and not just reacting, but strategizing. I don't know if he meant it as a game or life lesson—or maybe both—but it stuck with me. That board taught me how to slow down, focus, and play the long game. Side note: my brother-in-law used to tease me for my sweater vest collection, but if he'd seen Mr. Moore and understood where the inspo came from, man, he might've asked to borrow one. Love you, Mr. Moore.

Eighth grade brought me Mr. Sage (a name almost too perfect for a teacher, but also far too limiting). While his intelligence was evident, it was his character that taught me the most. Mr. Sage showed me what it meant to be a good man, and not just in a theoretical, classroom kind of way, but through consistent, intentional action. He lived the lessons he taught. At Chalmers, eighth graders had the opportunity to go on a class trip ahead of graduation, but there was a catch— we had to earn it. The trip wasn't free, and the school didn't have a budget that included a luxury allowance, so instead of forcing our parents to scrounge up the cash, the school set up a candy sales operation designed to help each student come up with the four-hundred dollars needed to cover transportation, lodging, meals, everything. It was a tall order, but we were up for the challenge.

Lord knows we were out there hustling. You couldn't walk a block without seeing one of us holding a box of candy bars, flashing million-watt smiles, and trying to make a sale. For many of us, this was our first real taste of what felt like a job, so we took it seriously. No freebies, IOUs, or tab-running. If you wanted a candy bar you had to pay for it *today*. Even the local gang members respected the grind, with some buying a few bars here and there just to support. Maybe it reminded them of who they once were, or maybe they just wanted to see kids doing some-thing positive for once. Whatever the reason, their quiet support spoke volumes.

I worked hard for that money. Real hard. Churches, corner stores, liquor stores, check-cashing joints. No place was safe from Teron on a candy mission. And once I had earned enough, I needed a secure place to keep the money until it was time to turn it in. Naturally, I chose the most logical option available to a twelve-year-old: I folded the bills as tight as I could, tucked them into my durag, and tied it down snug. No one was getting that money unless they were prepared to fight or outsmart me. And that's exactly what happened. The next morning, I woke up and it was gone. All of it. Every. Last. Penny.

I searched. I cried. I searched again. I cried some more. I was devastated—as if someone had kidnapped a loved one or killed the family pet. And deep down, I knew exactly who'd taken it. My mother had a reputation, and when drugs were involved nothing was off-limits. CDs, video games, gently worn clothes, could all be flipped for cash. While she denied it at the time, she eventually confessed—years later—that she'd taken the money and with it a piece of my spirit, sense of accomplishment, and the belief that hard work could lead to reward.

And to make matters worse, now I had to walk into Mr. Sage's classroom and tell him. I had to tell him that I no longer had the funds. That all my work had been for nothing. That I'd failed. I wasn't just afraid of his punishment, I was terrified of his disappointment. Of seeing that look in his eyes that said, "I expected more from you," but I did it anyway. I walked straight up to him, told the truth, and as I spoke I watched his face display what I thought was displeasure but came to understand it as something more daunting— pity. Sympathy. A kind of sadness that can only come from recognizing someone else's deeply complex pain and knowing there's no easy fix. To my surprise he didn't yell, reprimand, or shame. Instead, he listened, processed, and then discreetly sent me back to my desk.

Days passed and Mr. Sage said nothing more on the matter.

He went about teaching like normal, but I was spiraling: *Is he angry? Planning something? Has he written me off? Am I going to get expelled? Arrested? Oh no! I'm going to jail! I'm not ready for prison; I mean, I cried when I had to scrub off my washable tattoo because the rag was too rough. How am I gonna survive in jail? They're gonna eat me alive.* My imagination ran wild with worst-case scenarios. And then came the announcement:

"Teron Buford, please report to the principal's office. Teron Buford to the principal's office."

Oh, Lord. This was it. The hammer was about to drop. I walked slower than I ever had in my life, my personal form of protest. If I was about to be punished, they were going to wait for it. When I arrived I saw Dr. Blackburn (our principal), her admin, Mr. Sage, and one other familiar face: Uncle Mike. Turns out, Mr. Sage had *not* forgotten. Far from it. He and Uncle Mike had been quietly talking behind the scenes, trying to find a way to make things right. They both knew how hard I'd worked to afford the class trip and refused to let someone else's brokenness erase what I'd built. Uncle Mike reached into his wallet and pulled out two crisp hundred-dollar bills. I couldn't believe it. Mr. Sage reached into his wallet and pulled out two more. I nearly fell over.

In that moment, I learned more about dignity and citizenship than any textbook could ever teach. During that brief show of mercy and support, I learned there's a realm beyond empathy that puts feelings into action. For anyone wondering, I'd define empathy as being able to imagine what it's like to walk in someone else's shoes, which is admirable, but there's more that can be done to promote true and sustainable improved outcomes. That's where compassion comes in; doing something about the hurt by putting your time, talent, and resources on the table to ease someone else's suffering. Mr. Sage didn't just teach English or Social Studies, he instilled in us what it looks like to show up for people when it counts. To see them. To believe in them. He gave me a lesson in real manhood, resilience and what it means to lead with heart. Love you, Mr. Sage.

Toughen Up, Kid

N O CLEVER SUBTLETIES, CLICHÉS, or puns here: I hate bullies. Always have and always will. As an adult, there's something about being in a clear position to wield power or influence over someone else's day and actively choosing to cause harm instead of speaking life that sends my engine into overdrive. I can only see red as I execute the mental gymnastics routine needed to convince myself that the best way to practice compassion in the presence of such people is with swift, devastating, and indiscriminate force.

As a broke, scrawny and timid kid, however, I never had the courage or wherewithal to stand up for myself or others, which sometimes made me easy prey for the equally insecure and misguided ruffians in my neighborhood. By middle school I'd made new friends and discovered a belief in my academic ability, but I wasn't spared the burden of choosing between fighting back or, quite literally—taking it on the chin. At the time, the latter option seemed like the only one available to me.

While the four-year stay at our new apartment brought stability, it also came with little chance to reinvent myself. Though unsettling, hopping from school to school had its perks, affording me the chance to start fresh and seize the opportunity to reset the tone for who I wanted to be almost yearly, without the worry of someone calling out my contradictions. Not this time, though. There were no restarts, rebrands, or makeovers on the horizon. I'd become who I was going to be, and whatever reputation I'd built up was there to stay. While many of the boys I was beginning to socialize with were cultivating personas of popularity and athleticism with dreams of making it to the league, that wasn't the lens through which I was seen. My calling card was less visible but just as recognizable and tended to leave a lasting impression long after I'd exited the room. Vulnerable moment incoming...

Finances were tight and we'd become unnaturally familiar with compromising on luxuries like electricity, gas, or water because we usually didn't have the money to cover all of them. I hated the times when we opted for electricity, because that usually meant we'd be without hot water, which resulted in me occasionally missing a shower—or five—and re-wearing the same school uniform a time or two... or ten. Layer on recess, gym class, the natural movement of a twelve-year-old who couldn't sit still, and the newfound ability to produce a tangy aroma from one's armpits, and just like that, my brand was created. Teron Louis Buford: the dirty, musty kid who wore the same clothes every day. Toss in the occasional acne outbreak, the crackle that comes with a pubescent voice, unpredictable arousal when the cute classmate takes the seat right next to yours, and the incomparable horror of the teacher asking you to stand up and read aloud as you reckon with the reality of having pitched a pants tent that rivals the Washington Monument, and you've got all the ingredients needed to mix a stiff (pun intended) cocktail of insecurity and shame. Relative to the time, that was a tough season for me to weather as a kid.

Hormones aside, and taking full accountability for my disregard, I'll admit there were probably ways I could've done better with hygiene, but the unreliable access to basic utilities certainly didn't help. And man, the neighborhood kids and classmates let me hear about it. Though hurtful, it was to be expected; kids rag on each other all the time. That's what we do, but I wasn't ready for some of the other critics...

Ms. Shethead and Ms. DuMet—pronounced however you'd like, but I prefer "ShitHead" and "DumbAss"— seemed to really dislike me. I mean, I knew not every teacher was going to worship the ground I walked on, but those two couldn't stand me and weren't concerned with hiding it. One time Ms. Shethead told me straight to my face that she didn't think I'd ever amount to anything while also making not-so-veiled remarks about my hygiene. And though traumatizing, she wasn't the worst. Oh no. That honor goes, without question, to Ms. DuMet. She took the cake. In her seventh-grade math class she recognized that many of the boys (but not me, I swear) chose to hurl cruel, ill-hearted barbs at a girl whose circumstances mirrored mine, but as a young lady coming of age, she was much more aromatically betrayed by her lack of access to feminine hygiene products and inconsistent bathing. Let's call her Nicki. To her credit, Ms. DuMet initially came to Nicki's defense, admonishing the boys for their insensitive, crass, and scarring remarks. But then, she went a step further...in the wrong direction. She said, "...and y'all need to leave Nicki alone because we all know who the real stanky student is, and it ain't her," while looking directly at me with parsed lips, furrowed brows, and a face that suggested I was somehow to blame for *their* behavior and deserving of the spotlight she'd so maliciously placed on me. I'll always remember her words because, though there were a thousand other ways she could have redirected that moment, this thirty-something-year-old "educator" chose the one that weaponized it against me.

I. Hate. Bullies.

Unfortunately for me, being treated as a metaphorical (but sometimes literal) punching bag wasn't limited to school. I was never the biggest, strongest, or bravest kid in the neighborhood, which made me easy pickings for boys trying to make a name for themselves at the expense of someone else. In their defense, I don't think they saw it as bullying. To them, it was probably just about showing the strength they thought necessary to avoid being targeted themselves. *Manning up*. Survival. Kids being kids. Dog-eat-dog. I didn't care about the nomenclature. I just wanted it to stop. Thank goodness for Daz and MeMe.

I met them in fifth grade, and without those two, life would have been exponentially harder to navigate. Daz was two years older and MeMe had me by one. From the moment we unpacked the moving van at our new apartment through the day I left Chicago for good, they had my back. Whenever I went out, I was with them. We were as thick as thieves, bonded at the hip, and unwilling to let anyone or anything come between us. Looking back on all the harrowing moments we endured together, I can confidently say that having our small, loyal crew undoubtedly spared me more than a few beatings. Sure, there was that time MeMe got clocked in the eye during one of our many neighborhood rock fights. And yeah, I vividly remember when we got robbed at Douglas Park and had to give up Daz's brand-new bike in exchange for our safety. And there are probably a hundred other episodic adventures—each carrying its own lesson or warning—that I've since forgotten but, man, those were the days.

One thing remains as clear as the sky is blue: I loved those guys, and I probably wouldn't be here without them. Devastatingly, MeMe passed away before his fortieth birthday from a sudden asthma attack, and when that news broke, I was inconsolable. A young life interrupted, and I never took the chance to thank him for his friendship, loyalty, and protection. Damn. I'm sorry I didn't say this sooner, but love you, bro. Rest well, big homie.

Thug-Life

Anyone who knows today's iteration of Teron would probably find it hard to believe that there was once a darker version of him; a kid who nearly veered down a path he might not have returned from. But before we get into that alternate timeline, let's do a little math: poor kid living in a resource desert + shy Black boy who wasn't particularly loud or outspoken + constantly picked-on kid who didn't want to fight back = desperation. It's not hard to see how gang life might appeal to someone in that equation. When you come from nothing, are surrounded by even less, and yearn for *something*, your brain starts looking for easy outs or shortcuts to get there. And for me, it wasn't about money or clout; I was looking for safety. Daz and MeMe

WHAT IF I'M ENOUGH?

had my back, no doubt, but I also understood their limitations. I needed something more. Something that'd keep me safe while simultaneously sending the message, "Don't mess with me."

It all came to a head during the break between seventh and eighth grade. By then, both Daz and MeMe had graduated from Chalmers, and I no longer had the same access to my guys. I had to find a new way to stay off the radar and I needed to do it fast. That same summer, I joined a traveling baseball team. I had no idea how fun it could be or how good I might become with the right coaching and some actual work ethic. Only problem— our home diamond was on the other side of Douglass Park, which meant I had to pass through rival gang territory just to get there. Didn't matter that I wasn't affiliated, my zip code spoke for me. Just living in the wrong neighborhood was enough to get you checked. I needed protection.

So, in the most awkward and unnatural way imaginable, I started trying to... well... get involved. Even writing that sentence sounds more like I was signing up for the PTA than flirting with gang culture, but that's how off-brand it was for me. Still, I tiptoed toward it. My neighborhood gang was always recruiting, and younger kids made ideal candidates because they usually flew under the radar of police. All I had to do was go through initiation.

"Teron, what's initiation?" Glad you asked. Initiation for this particular gang meant getting jumped by several members for a set amount of time, and if your body could endure the beating, you were in. I'm not sure if they wanted to see if you had the strength for the road ahead or if it was just their way of releasing their own pain veiled as toughness or masculinity. Regardless, the process was simple. Brutal, but simple. And I thought I was ready. That was, until Geo stepped in. Geo was an older kid in the neighborhood and one of the gang's junior leaders who secretly looked out for me. I don't know what he saw in me, but I'll never forget what he said the day I stepped up to the stomping grounds: "Ay, shawty. This ain't for you. Go home."

Welp. Say less. That was all I needed to hear. I was out of there so fast you'd have thought I was training for the Olympics. Had I been thinking, I would've asked for an official time; my acceleration off the blocks would've at least qualified me for a lower-tier track scholarship. But the truth is, Geo's words unlocked something I already knew deep down, I wasn't gang material. I just didn't want to be a target anymore. That's it. I dreamed of having a two percent slice of what my cousin Tubby had—may he rest in peace. He was so well-loved in his neighborhood that nobody ever bothered or stepped to him, moving when he came through and thinking twice before disrespectful words left their mouths. And I wasn't asking for much. I didn't want to be feared, I just wanted peace. A little bit of space to exist without being harassed. Was that really too much to ask?

Lisa

Despite my best efforts, there are still parts of my story I struggle to talk about. Not because I'm unwilling, but because I literally don't know where to place them. They don't fit neatly. They hang in the air, remaining hard to revisit. Not just because they're painful, but because of the role I played in them. Now, you might be thinking, "How could this possibly get more complicated?" Oh, trust me. It can. I haven't even told you about Lisa or the gun.

When I was twelve years old, I met Lisa. She was the daughter of a close family friend, so we spent a lot of time together. Probably too much. Lisa was about a year and a half younger than me. Like kids everywhere else, we acted out our screwed-up, half-understood versions of adulthood; copying what they saw in music videos or heard in half-whispered conversations from older cousins.

Lisa and I weren't any different. We flirted and played games we had no business playing, like "hide-n-go-freak" (not seek), where if you were caught, you had to dry hump the person who found you. Gross, I know, but it was common. That's what kids my age were doing. Everyone was supposedly "doing it," and based on the way folks told their stories, I was one of the last seventh graders left who hadn't "gone all the way."

One night, Lisa and her mom stayed over at our apartment, and since we were both just kids (as they say), nobody thought twice about us sharing a bed. There were six or seven of us packed into that place anyway, what could possibly go wrong? Well... things escalated. What began as a little footsie turned into a whole lot more. Next thing I knew we were on the living room floor, and she was on top of me. I was terrified, but Lisa knew enough for the both of us, moving with a kind of confidence and experience that felt... advanced. Way beyond our years. By the time I realized I wasn't ready—mentally, emotionally, spiritually—it was already too late. I'd "become a man" right as I realized boyhood was more suitable.

The Gun

MeMe and I were walking through the alley behind my apartment when he showed me a toy gun his older brother had picked up. It was a BB gun styled like a forty-five-millimeter pistol, but the orange safety tip had been removed, making it look way too real. I begged MeMe to let me hold it. When he finally gave in, I admiringly walked with it in my hand, marveling at its weight and detail and thinking how real it felt. But something in my gut was… off. I couldn't shake the feeling that we were being watched. I turned around and there it was, a cop car. Creeping up from behind and surveilling our every move. I didn't run because I knew I wasn't supposed to, but nobody said I couldn't speed-walk.

I turned the corner and picked up the pace, hoping that if I broke line of sight I could stash the thing and maybe avoid the whole situation altogether. No luck. The cruiser sped up to close the gap. Why didn't I just toss it into a yard or drop it when I had the chance? Stupid 'tween. I rounded the last corner. One turn away from what I thought would be my safe haven. *Yes!* I silently celebrated. *I made it to my front porch and Granny's outside. She'll protect me. She always protects me.* That's when the lights hit and the siren wailed.

I immediately froze in place as the officer—a massive white man who looked about nine feet tall and seven-hundred pounds—got out of the car and approached me without saying a word and began to pat me down. Granny jumped up, yelling, "Why are you bothering my baby!? What did he do!?" Still silent, Officer Ogre pulled the gun from my waistband and held it up for her to see. She paused for a moment to weigh her options before decisively responding, "...ah, well go ahead and take him to jail then."

Granny, I thought, *You're supposed to be my ride-or-die! You're just gonna let him take me!?—* As if she had a say in the matter. But here's the twist, he didn't arrest me. Instead he took the gun, looked me square in the eyes and said something I'll never forget, "Son, if I were a different officer and this were a different day, you might not have made it out of this situation." He walked back to his squad car, plopped down into the driver seat, slammed the door, and before pulling away, gave me one piece of free advice, "Make better decisions." That was it. Make. Better. Decisions. And you know what? I still think about those three words, attempting to live by them to this very day.

GUARDIAN ANGELS

N OT EVERYONE WAS AS fortunate as I was as a kid. I know how absurd that sounds given the story you've read up to this point, but I mean that from the bottom of my heart and with my whole chest. Yeah, I had all sorts of tragedy and challenge, but I also had something that many others in similar situations didn't. Pillars. You know, those super-sturdy supports that don't bend or break easily, no matter how much weight you place on them. Where some had none, I had plenty. They couldn't always save me from myself, but I knew they'd be there when I needed them most.

Grandma Nancy and Grandpa TC

With my dad being in and out of my life so unpredictably, I didn't really spend a ton of time around his side of the family. Sure, there were BBQs here and there, maybe a small birthday party, but nothing meaningful or consistent. Well… except for Grandma Nancy and Grandpa TC. While I didn't see them regularly, I could always count on two times a year when they showed up. Thanksgiving and Christmas.

On Thanksgiving morning, Grandpa would ride around the city in a large passenger van, picking up all the grandchildren

and busing us to their house in a suburb about forty-five minutes outside the city. In my memory, there were no fewer than
twenty-five kids in the back of the van. All of us playing, arguing,
and trying to stay awake through what felt like parking-lot-lev-
el traffic. We'd pull up and Grandma Nancy would already be
cooking up a storm: turkey, ham, dressing (not stuffing; I'm a
nice guy, but I *will* fight you on this), cornbread, deviled eggs,
sweet potato pie, pound cake, cranberry sauce, and that lus-
cious, gooey, unmistakable baked macaroni and cheese (with
egg. Argue with ya momma, not me). My sisters would hang out
in the kitchen watching her cook, asking about recipes but never
getting a straight answer as she'd always reply with something
like, "a little bit of this and a pinch of that." Grandma didn't need
measuring cups; she added ingredients until she heard a soft
whisper from our ancestors say, *Enough, my child.*

They had this huge table that could seat a thousand people, and everyone would be sitting around eating and laughing to their heart's content. (Okay, I might be misremember-
ing the size of the table, but I was a kid. Cut me some slack,
please. I'm in my feelings). We'd eat and play, eat and play
again, and then crash around 8:00 p.m. Grandpa would drive
us back the next day, each of us carrying a plate of whatever
hadn't been devoured the night before. Of course, with all those
mouths in our apartment, leftovers didn't last long. But hey,
that's what happens when you play the high-stakes game of
hoarding-food-while-broke.

Christmas was the same deal. Grandpa made rounds the day
before while Grandma cooked all through the night. The only
difference? On Christmas morning, we'd wake up to what felt

like hundreds of gifts under the tree. It seemed like each of the two dozen kids walked away with at least ten presents, and for a few precious hours we were given the go-ahead to pretend like everything in life was okay. No worrying about the next meal. No stress over whether the heat would get turned off. Grandma Nancy and Grandpa TC gave us our childhoods, if only for a couple nights a year.

As I grew older, my relationship with them only deepened. I came to better understand their brand of quick-witted love, sage wisdom, and direct confrontation and condemnation of anything that resembled bad behavior. And while I'm a little ashamed to admit it, it took me decades to realize that the greatest and most cherished gifts they ever gave us didn't come wrapped in shiny bows and they weren't gently placed under an immaculately decorated tree. They were the lessons they subliminally implanted into our subconscious minds that lasted far longer than the life expectancy of that remote-controlled car or lightbulb-powered dessert oven.

Granny

Where do I begin? Grandma Beatrice, better known as Granny, was more like a mother than a grandmother. For as long as I can remember I was with her, and for as long as I draw breath, she'll be with me. My mom and dad had a little apartment for themselves in the early years before moving into a duplex shortly after, but I was always with Granny. Almost everything I know and everything I am can be traced back to her. When I was maybe five or six years old, Granny had this huge house on the West Side of Chicago. Her husband, Isaac, had passed away years before I was born, leaving her with that entire space to manage on her own. "Luckily" for her, a handful of her seven children never ventured far from the nest, leaving her to play den mother to a bunch of adults who all had kids of their own. And so began the tradition of packing dozens of people into Granny's home.

Man, that woman was an angel and she loved her some Jesus. Every morning around 6:00 a.m., she'd say the same prayer, thanking God for waking her up before proceeding to ask Him to take the taste of drugs out of folks' mouths, give people the strength to seek His face, keep the children safe on the streets, and bless everyone with their basic needs. Every night around 10:00 p.m., she'd do it all over again, this time thanking God for all He'd done that day and asking for safe passage into the next (if it be His will). I know this because almost every single time she prayed, I was right there next to her. On my knees, listening as she recited what felt like a two-hour-long prayer twice a day.

When I tell you Granny was a God-fearing, God-loving, church-going woman, I need you to believe me. She spent so much time at our home church you would've thought she was part-owner. Bible Study? She was there. Choir rehearsal? There. Daily scripture study? She did that at home, but yeah, she was there too. Around 6:00 p.m. every Saturday, Granny and I would turn on one of the AM gospel stations and listen as the greats sang hymns to prepare us for what I can only describe as the marathon that was our Sunday mornings and afternoons.

The church van would pick us up and drop us off at our place of worship's front doors by 7:00 a.m. each Sunday, just in time for Early Morning Prayer Band. Basically, a group of church elders would gather to send out prayers for those in urgent need of blessing and care. That ran until about 8:00 a.m., at which point they'd take a break from praying to grab a little nourishment in the church's kitchen.

That breakfast was hitting! I always got the same thing: grits, eggs, sausages, and a biscuit. I'd mix the grits with a little bit of egg before making my own version of a sausage, egg, and cheese biscuit sandwich. While breakfast wasn't technically free, they'd let you eat if you were there and hungry. Trying to live that *What Would Jesus Do?* lifestyle, Granny always tossed a little cash in the pot, partly because she wanted to help keep the church running, and partly because she got tired of the kitchen staff giving me side-eye when I couldn't scrounge up the "suggested donation" posted at the register. Saintly, right?

At 9:00 a.m., we'd separate. She went to adult Sunday School while I went to the kids' version. I should mention this church was massive, so I'd try to sneak away from breakfast around 8:45 a.m. to hang out with my friends before class started. We'd push each other around in wheeled chairs, play hide and seek, truth or dare, or whatever game we could make up to work out our wiggles before the adults walked in and demanded our attention.

At 10:30 a.m., it was time for church service. I'd spend the first hour in children's church where we heard a parallel sermon to whatever was being preached in "big church." Then, after that first hour, all the kids would rejoin their families for the remainder of the service. Yes, you heard that correctly, the remainder. You know, for someone so God-fearing, our pastor sure did lie a lot. Always saying, "Give me just a few more minutes and I'ma get y'all outta here." Yeah, okay. Fool me once, shame on you. Fool me twice...then you can't get fooled again. (little presidential humor for those who get it).

I'd walk in and see Granny sitting in her usual seat, singing and testifying at the top of her lungs. "Hallelujah! Amen! You better preach! Yes, Lord!" I told you, Granny loved her some Jesus. And she was, as the Bible prefers, a cheerful giver. The congregation would read the Tithers' Covenant, which was basically a call-and-response series of scriptures prompting followers to give ten percent of their earnings to the church. After that, they'd pass the collection plates for the general offering. Then the benevolent offering. Then the building fund offering. And on special occasions, the pastor's anniversary offering or some other collection. It didn't matter how many plates came around or how many causes needed support, Granny always had something to give.

Pastor ended each service with an invitation. If you'd been touched by the spirit but hadn't yet been baptized, this was your moment. You were invited to stand up, proclaim Jesus Christ as your Lord and Savior, and wade into the water. I still remember the day I raised my hand and walked to the front of the church. I looked back at Granny, and I had never seen her so proud. In truth, I was doing it more for her than for myself. I knew she wanted me to give my life to God, but the church wouldn't authorize it unless I asked. As a well-versed and efficient little sinner, I expected to disintegrate or burst into flames when I hit that holy water, but aside from a bit of burning in the eyes, I came out intact. And when I emerged from the baptismal pool, there was Granny, front and center, tears streaming down her face.

As I've grown, I've seen some of the terrible, inhumane things people have done in the name of God, justified by using a random verse or two taken wildly out of context two thousand years later, and as a result, I've become less connected with today's version of organized religion. I often find myself wondering if Granny's still proud of me despite having stepped back from church in its more traditional form. I'd like to think so, and maybe I'll get the chance to ask her one day. I mean, I still believe there's a higher power out there. I just don't think it looks like a surfer bro, is only able to bless America, or hates poor, queer, or brown people.

Outside of church, Granny's lovingly fierce demeanor had a magnetic hold on me. It never mattered what was going on or how much we struggled, I was always there by her side, and she was always there by mine. A walking anomaly, she was the first person I'd ever seen stand up to my dad in defense of my mother. Yet, at the same time I'd witnessed her children use and abuse her without her ever calling it out, cutting them off, or holding it against them. Thirty and forty-something-year-olds still milking off their mother, stealing from her already limited and fixed income to buy drugs, expecting her to cook meals, asking her to sacrifice so they didn't have to make hard calls. They'd curse her out, call her names, and make her feel like the worst mother ever when she couldn't (or wouldn't) feed their habits. It must've hurt her deeply, but you'd never have known it based on the way she optimistically floated through life.

In July of 2002 Granny had become really sick. I mean, she'd been ailing before, but this was different. She'd suffered a few heart attacks and now required round-the-clock care as she re-covered. The adults tried to keep this information from the kids for as long as possible, but we knew something was wrong. She went to live with Uncle Mike on the South Side since he was the only one who had the access and means to take care of her.

Around September or October, Uncle Mike came over to our apartment (still in Granny's name, even though she was no longer living there) and asked if anyone wanted to visit her at his house. A couple of people hopped into his car, which left one seat remaining for me. "Nah, let someone else go instead" I said, because I was busy having fun with my friends. I could always go see her another time, right?

On November 5, 2002, I went out to play basketball at the park with the homies one last time before the winter chill set in. It was unseasonably warm, perfect hoops weather, and let me tell you, I was out there GETTING BUCKETS. I was on fire. We must've played from the time school let out until maybe 7:00 p.m. My team never lost a game, and I even almost got my first dunk! Out of the blue and extremely uncharacteristically, my dad pulled up to the park and told me to get in the car with my sisters already in the back seat. He drove us to his apartment over on Sixteenth Street, but all I remember from the ride was how many stars there were in the sky. I didn't think anything of it, but it was an amazing sight to see. We pulled up around 7:30 p.m. and did the usual afterschool stuff: homework, argued, played a few games, ate a little something. Then dad called us all into his room and broke the news. Granny had passed away late that afternoon, which to me, perfectly explained the abnormal number of visible stars in the night sky. My sisters immediately burst into tears, but I didn't. I didn't feel sad, or mad, or grief. I felt... nothing. I was numb. In shock.

I went to lie down, and that's when it set in— Granny was gone and never coming back. The woman who'd been there for me through everything would never sing another hymn, mend another wound, or watch another episode of cartoons with me. The pillow quickly turned into a sponge. I remember thinking, though many others had passed away before her, this was the first time a death actually impacted me. That thought, and grief, were immediately and substantially complicated further by the unrelenting and punishing words that played on repeat in my head: *I can't believe I didn't go visit her. I had a chance to see her one more time and didn't because I was too busy goofing around outside.*

Like most classic Black movies, when the shepherd dies, the flock scatters. We were no different. After the funeral we were evicted from the apartment and left searching not only for a new home, but a new sense of meaning. Granny was gone, and with her went any semblance of identity or familial connection. Cousins I'd quite literally grown up with faded away, not by any fault of their own though, it just... happened. My younger sisters went to live with my dad for about a month while my mom stayed with a friend. MeMe's grandmother let me crash at their place while I planned my next move. And though it took a little time and reflection, a lightbulb eventually went off in my mother's head— *I gotta get outta here.* She couldn't stand the idea of staying in the city that reminded her of her shortcomings, struggled to live in a place haunted by the loss of her mother, and grew tired of the constant peril she found herself in. So, almost in the blink of an eye, she packed up my sisters with little more than the clothes on their backs, hopped on a Greyhound bus, and headed to Minnesota while I stayed behind in Chicago. I wasn't ready to leave, and the homeless shelter they ended up in didn't permit boys my age to stay there anyway. So, in a strange way that only makes sense in the head of a stubborn and thoughtless fourteen-year-old, it was a win-win situation.

Uncle Mike

A few years before Granny passed away, my mom pulled me aside for a walk around our neighborhood. "Teron, I know how much you love your uncle, so I need to tell you something." I was confused and scared as I anxiously wondered what could possibly be so important that she had to take me around the block just to say it.

"Okay... shoot," I managed.

"Well, your uncle loves you. You know that, right? Right? I just need you to know that Uncle Mike is gay and has HIV." I'll never forget the look on her face as she forced those words out, watching me closely for my reaction. "Uh, okay..." I replied. Partly because I didn't really know what that meant, but also because it didn't change anything for me. Uncle Mike was Uncle Mike. It didn't matter who he loved or what challenges he faced, I'd always love him. Nothing could ever change that. EVER.

Before my mom left for Minnesota, she arranged for me to stay with him after he'd moved into a small house in Oak Brook, IL, a rich suburb about a half-hour west of the city. He'd worked for the Chicago Transit Authority for nearly thirty years and had made his way up the ranks, earning a good living and he wasn't shy about sharing it. He was quick to give, buying friends and family designer accessories, clothes, even cars. He wasn't afraid to swipe that card, that's for dang sure. And my dude could not resist a good swap meet or deal. Like, "Uncle Mike, do you really need that knock-off Gucci pencil sharpener?"

"Yeah, boy! It's half off!"

He enrolled me in the local public high school, which was made up of several buildings connected via skyway, multiple fields for extracurricular activities, and a pool (because, why wouldn't it?). Looking more like a small college campus, I remember thinking— *Oh, so this is where rich people send their kids? No metal detectors at the doors. No armed police in the hallways. These people must really trust the students, huh?* The classrooms were pristine, filled with the latest tech. The cafeteria was like a food court. The teachers seemed joyful, never tired or worn out. And the students? For the most part, friendly... but also very, very White. People often fail to mention how segregated Chicago is. My old neighborhood? All Black. But if you crossed the major intersection near the projects, it was all Latinx. And we never, EVER mixed. Not out of hate, it's just how things were. So when I moved out to the 'burbs with Uncle Mike, I encountered (you guessed it) my first White classmate. Took me fifteen years, but it finally happened. It was at this very same time, unfortunately, that I began a decades-long struggle with authentic identity, mental health, and self-love. But more about that later.

Uncle Mike worked odd hours and wanted me to be self-sufficient and ready for whatever this new, strange, and affluent land might throw at me. On day one he handed me a box of condoms and gave me a long lecture. And when I say box, I don't mean a twelve-pack from the local pharmacy. I mean shoebox-sized with at least three dozen condoms in every shape, size, color, and flavor imaginable (hey, don't judge my uncle!). I reassured him I wouldn't need them but thanked him anyway. He schooled me on how people in the suburbs operated, using it as an excuse to feed his obsession with looking, feeling, and smelling good regardless of the financial toll. He kept me in name-brand clothes and made sure I never went without, even buying me a PlayStation 2 (the hottest console at the time), giving me a credit card, setting me up with a budget, and pretending not to notice when I overspent. It didn't take long for this poor city boy to get real bougie. Like—*Would you like some iced tea? Yes, but could you add a splash of lemon and serve it in a chilled glass? Please and thank you*— levels of bougie.

But ultimately, Uncle Mike really only wanted me to be prepared for the realistic and feasible trials that life might throw at me. Hard conversations, tough lessons, and small trials here and there encompassed his brand of age-appropriate education, which might seem odd to some but had a lasting impact on me. Heck, Uncle Mike even gave me my first drink. "Skillz" (that was his nickname for me), he said, "If you're gonna be out here partying with these rich kids, I need you to know your limits."

Now, despite everything I'd lived through up until this point, I was a total fraidy cat. I'd never tried anything. Even when I sat in a circle with friends passing around a blunt, I never actually smoked. I'd blow into the tip to make it look like I was taking a puff while pretending to grow ever more lit with each pull. I was as square as could be. But I trusted Uncle Mike. So, I took the glass and sipped.

My inner monologue was off the chain! *Oh my God. What is this? Lighter fluid? Diesel fuel? Liquid death?!* "How do you feel?" he asked. My first thought was to tell him how it was the most disgusting thing I'd ever tasted and that it felt like I'd swallowed a razor blade that gave birth to fire demons in my stomach who were frantically attempting to climb back up through my throat and redeposit themselves into the glass from which they came, which now sat untouched on the table. Attempting to save face, however, I simply replied, "you know what, I'm good on drinking. I don't think it's for me." A promise I've kept to this day. Turns out, Uncle Mike had poured me a shot of some crazy-strong malt liquor, hoping I'd think twice before ever trying alcohol again. Dude was a genius. A devious, bougie, loving, genius.

Love you, Uncle Mike.

Aunt Gloria

With Uncle Mike working so much, I was often home alone. That's when I started honing my cooking skills and drastically improving my hygiene, but after a while there's only so much experimenting you can do in the kitchen and so many hours you can spend mindlessly playing video games before restlessness kicks in. Thankfully, I had family just a mile and a half away. Aunt Gloria opened her home to me, and I'll forever be grateful to her for it.

And let me tell you, this lady wasn't just welcoming, she was a force. She had a way of commanding the room without having to raise her voice and her presence was equal parts comforting and electrifying. One moment she'd slice through tension with a sharp one-liner that left everyone doubled over in laughter, and the next she'd drop a piece of wisdom that stuck with you long after the conversation ended. She could weave humor and truth together so seamlessly that you couldn't help but grow from being around her. And when the music was on—those old school R&B records she loved—you felt like you were stepping into her personal sanctuary. That's where I first understood how music could carry both tenderness and power, something I'd later lean on when love or apology called for more than just words.

Aunt Gloria's home was also where I developed and deepened my relationships with beloved family members like Aunt Ro, Cousin Miranda, Johnny, Fray, NeNe, and all the other aunts, uncles, and play cousins. But beyond that, Aunt Gloria provided me a symbolic portal into a world of second-chance with Granny. Not only did she physically resemble my late grandmother, she carried her spirit. And I think that combination played a big role in the bond we formed. She'd tell me stories about how much Granny loved me while sprinkling in her own reflections of my childhood, recounting instances of present-day accomplishments and her pride in the fact that I hadn't let my past struggles dim my future potential. She was the warm hug I didn't even know I needed back then but do now. Love you, Aunt Gloria and all who descend from her.

No Place Like Home(less)

I N MAY 2004, I got a phone call from my mom. Though I'd spent the last year and a half building a new life with Uncle Mike, she said it was time for me to join her in Minnesota. Despite our history, I loved my mother and missed regularly seeing my baby sisters, but I was nowhere near ready to leave behind everything I'd cultivated in such a short time. I begged and pleaded to stay, arguing that I had earned the right to have my input weighed equally. After all, I was nearly a grown man. I mean, come on... sixteen times around the sun and a whole lot of lived experience, that should count for something, right? Now, you— the reasonable, thoughtful reader—probably agree that there's absolutely no downside to letting an emotionally-charged and obviously impartial teen make life-altering decisions with no oversight. My mother and Uncle Mike, however, didn't share your enlightened perspective. They don't appreciate you, but I do. I. Do.

I swam in the deepest depths of despair and denial, vowing to anyone who'd listen that I'd be back as quickly as I was forced to leave. I said tearful goodbyes to the life I'd just come to know, boarded the cramped interstate bus, and begrudgingly made the eight-hour trip to what I was convinced would be a hellish new chapter in Minneapolis, MN. Man, I don't think I'd ever hated my mother more than I did while staring out that fingerprint-smudged window, watching the countryside blur by. I spent the entire ride crafting elaborate, petty narratives about why she'd really called me back.

It must've been a flex... or a spite move because Uncle Mike didn't send her money or disagreed with her on something trivial, I imagined. Or Maybe she just wanted to feel some sense of control over me, and you can't do that from four hundred miles away, right? Wrong. Not you, me. I was wrong. It took nearly twenty years, but like my holier-than-thou elders used to say when they sensed lies in the air, the truth always comes out. As much as I wanted my mother to be the villain in my superhero origin story, the reality was that she'd been protecting me all along. She took the blame for a decision she didn't make, because Uncle Mike was planning to move back to the South Side of Chicago at the end of the school year, and fearing I might fall in with the wrong crowd, she sent for me. She saved me. And since I didn't know any better, I hated her for it. When I asked her, years later, why she kept the truth from me, she sighed and admitted that she didn't want me to resent Uncle Mike, the closest thing I'd had to a father in a long time. So, she took the hit and covered for him.

Shortly before I arrived, my mother and sisters had been placed in transitional housing. The program allowed me to join them as she worked on developing life skills, managing a small budget, saving up emergency cash, and eventually getting placed in stable, affordable housing within the year. My mother had come to universally distrust inner-city public schools, so she enrolled me in a suburban one on the edge of Minneapolis. We didn't own a car, but (un)fortunately for me, the school district arranged for a bus to pick me up right in front of the shelter as its last stop before heading to school. A bus full of insecure teenagers. Picking up the homeless kid. From the shelter. What could possibly go wrong? No shade to anyone experiencing homelessness, but I know how cruel kids can be. I'd just gotten my first taste of non-bullied life, and now I was about to dive right back in after only a couple years of peace. How is that fair?

Educated

THE SUMMER I MOVED to Minnesota, I learned a lot about the bubble I came from and the beauty of difference. I took my sisters to Elliot Park almost every day where they'd run around with their friends and push each other on the swings while I spent hours playing pick-up ball. I wasn't exactly Hall of Fame material, but I held my own. I had a decent shot and some solid bounce, averaging two or three dunks a game, and while they counted just the same as layups, there was something about elevating over an opponent, throwing one down through contact, flexing hard, and sprinting back on defense that just hit differently. My ego was ballooning. I was feeling myself so much that I even challenged the big homie, "G," to a dunk-off.

The rules were simple: the offensive player started at the three-point line, defender under the basket. On the count of three, the offensive player would go up strong, trying to dunk while the defender did their best to block it. Being the scholar and gentleman he was, G let me go first. I gripped the ball like it owed me money, sprinted in with everything I had, and launched toward the hoop. I went up. G went up. I went higher. G went higher. I cocked the ball back like a slingshot. G raised his arm. I swung the ball forward with all my might and even more confidence. G blocked it without breaking a sweat, sending it flying thirty feet toward the bleachers. Red flag number one. Now, I know what you're thinking: *Teron, that should've been the end of it. You should've taken your L and sat down.* Nope. There were too many cuties on the sidelines who just witnessed my humiliation. I had to reclaim my honor.

G's turn. Instead of starting outside the three-point arc, he confidently planted himself just past the free throw line, boasting he'd "only need one step to get it done." Red flag number two. Oblivious to the outcome you can already see coming, dear reader, I got into position, ready to return the embarrassment handed to me mere moments earlier. One. Two. Three. Go! G took one power dribble and propelled himself into the sky. He went up. I went up. So far, so good. G kept rising. I did the same. No big deal. G elevated even higher, as if he had pressed a hidden nitrous oxide button on the ball that activated tiny rockets on his shoes. I… plateaued. Red flag number three. Realizing he was about to completely leapfrog me, G casually placed his left hand on the back of my head and guided it between his split-apart legs, throwing down the nastiest dunk Elliot Park had ever seen before calling NASA to request permission to land. Smiling as he re-entered Earth's atmosphere and adding insult to injury by helping me up off the ground that was momentarily serving as my hospital bed, G dusted me off and applauded my good try. Joke's on him, though. Sure, I got dunked on *once*, but he got rug burn on *both* balls as his scrotum skipped across the top of my scalp. Scoreboard. *You* tell *me* who won.

My run in with G wouldn't be the last time I was taught a lesson in humility on the basketball court. In fact, the blacktop where I'd learned to pick my battles more wisely ended up being the same place where I got my first lessons in intercultural awareness and racial identity. One of my regular teammates was a super light-skinned dude who jokingly referred to himself as "damn near see-through." Let's call him Caden. We'd played so many games together that we couldn't help but get to know each other. We gradually started swapping pieces of our stories. I told him about life in Chicago and how I was adjusting to the shelter while he shared his experience growing up in a multiracial household— Black father, White mother. My mind was blown. *People can marry outside their race? Isn't that frowned upon?* Remember, I came from a deeply segregated part of Chicago where even knowing someone of another race was rare, let alone dating them. That concept was as foreign to me as nuclear physics.

One day, during a game, Caden lobbed me an alley-oop from near half-court. I caught and dunked it so hard I thought I'd broken a bone in my hand. As I jogged back to high-five him, he shouted, "Ay, my nigga got hops!" I froze. Like a deer in headlights. *Was that a compliment? I think it was a compliment? It felt like a compliment... but also didn't?* I didn't know how to process. On the one hand, he wasn't lying, I *did* have hops and it felt nice to be acknowledged. On the other hand, I didn't know which part of him had said it, the White or Black half. Cut me some slack, y'all. I now know how ignorant that sounds, but at the time, it made perfect sense to split his personhood in two. Like if someone offered him tuna fish casserole and collard greens, he'd freeze, caught between two irreconcilable worlds. Looking back, it's clear I had a lot to learn about identity and the complexities that tend to accompany it when it intersects with societal norms, traditions, preconceptions, and unadulterated ignorance.

And then there was Abdul, a Somali American kid who had recently immigrated to the U.S. We were talking about how strange it felt to move from one place to another (though, his transition was probably a bit more jarring than mine) when I made a comment that sparked tension. "Hey," I said, "we might not call this place home, but us brothers, we gotta stick together. It ain't easy being Black in America, and it's even harder doing it alone." Big mistake. Abdul immediately corrected me: he was Somali American, not Black. To Abdul (and many others) there's a stark difference between Africans who immigrate to America and American-born descendants of African slaves. Being labeled one or the other carried cultural weight, and in his view to be lumped in as "Black" meant accepting all the assumptions and stereotypes that came with it. In trying to build solidarity, I unintentionally stepped on a live wire, one that still divides immigrant and American-born Africans to this day. Decades later, I wonder if those distinctions were planted in our communities on purpose to create distance where there should have been unity. You know what they say about a house divided.

Modern Non-Fiction, Por Favor

I won't bore you with a play-by-play of my last two years of high school. I'll just say this: all that worry about being the homeless kid? Wasted energy. Nobody really cared. In fact, the few people who knew about my situation actually thought it was kind of cool that I was trying to beat the odds. Spoken like folks who clearly never had to fight for a meal or get food from the church pantry, but hey, I won't hold it against them. They weren't judging me, so I extended the same courtesy to them. By the end of the day, I was just another self-absorbed teenager: I pretended to be dumber than I was to fit in with other smart kids who were also downplaying their intelligence. I liked girls who didn't like me back. I failed to recongnize when someone was interested in me because I was too dense to do the social math. I thought I was cooler and cleverer than I actually was. And the pressure of figuring out my "what's next" was beginning to mount.

The summer before senior year, we moved into affordable housing in St. Paul, MN. By then, I had found my groove—academically and socially—and refused to transfer to a fourth high school in as many years. After talking it through with my mom, I decided to re-enroll into the school I'd attended the year prior, but that meant I'd lose access to a dedicated school bus and would have to figure out how to get across two cities on my own. Fortunately, I was already familiar with the metro transit system and had prepared an itinerary so "easy" to follow that almost anyone could work it out:

Catch the 21 from the corner of Selby and Victoria. Hop off at University and Snelling and wait fifteen minutes for the 16 or the express 50 from St. Paul to Minneapolis. Get off at Marquette and Second Avenue and decide whether to walk nine blocks to Nicollet and Tenth Street or catch the 10, and then wait another thirty minutes for the 63, which would drop me off about two blocks from the school's front door. All I had to do was be awake by 4:36 a.m. to catch the first bus at 5:29 a.m., ensuring I'd arrive before the 7:47 a.m. start time. After school activities, basketball or football commitments? Just do it all in reverse and make it home by 11:00 p.m. Easy. I'd do homework on the ride and get to know the bus drivers so well they'd let me catch a nap before waking me at my stop. I did that every day of senior year, and while you would think that my grades should have taken a hit, I had a couple benevolent teachers who met me halfway and helped pull me across the finish line: "Profé" and "Mr. Pointe."

Profé was my Spanish teacher during those last two years. She must've seen something in me because it felt like she was always looking out, pushing me to grow, challenging me to stretch, and finding ways to keep me involved. When she learned I was commuting from St. Paul and waking up before dawn, she checked in regularly to make sure I wasn't burning out. If I was going to be late, she found ways to help me catch up so I didn't fall behind. And when she discovered I didn't have the funds to pay my college housing and confirmation deposits, she helped me secure the resources to cover them. She was patient, flexible, and empathetic when she didn't have to be. I'm sure she'd worked with plenty of students facing hardship and could've easily grown numb to it, but she hadn't. She saw my inherent dignity and extended a hand when I needed it most. Love you, Profé.

Mr. Pointe was my English teacher, and when I met him, he was deep into his journey of social awareness and racial identity. I remember him telling our class about a conference he'd attended in Philly, where he was challenged to reflect on how race and skin tone shaped his everyday interactions. I didn't recognize it at the time, but looking back, I was incredibly proud of him. Here he was: a middle-aged White man sharing a vulnerable story with a room full of teenage knuckleheads, modeling what it looks like to grow beyond a narrow worldview. He made it clear that no matter your age or status, there's always room to learn and evolve, using his platform as an educator to ensure we understood the complexities of identity and intersectionality.

And here's the best part, if it weren't for Mr. Pointe, I might have never met my wife. Right before graduation, I told him I'd be attending a small private college in St. Paul, MN, and in response, he looked me in the eye, put his hands on my shoulders, and said, "Hey, that's a really White school. Make sure you meet as many Black folks as you can or you're gonna have a rough time." Mr. Pointe had never steered me wrong before, so I took him seriously, going on to create a social media account and friend-request every Black student in the college's network. The first one to accept? Dee. My future girlfriend-turned-wife. That's all you, Mr. Pointe. Love you, sir.

LESSONS LEARNED PART 2

Talk about fortunate breaks. If it weren't for Geo, I probably would've joined a gang and wound up dead or in jail before I turned eighteen. Mr. Jazzner recommended me for a spot at a prestigious college's two-week, on-campus camp for seventh graders who showed promise in mathematics. Mr. Sage encouraged two other students and me to enter the "Know Your Heritage Bowl," which landed us round-trip tickets to Orlando, FL, to compete at the national level. My grandparents watched over me when I thought I was all alone. Uncle Mike took me in when I had nowhere else to go. Aunt Gloria, Aunt Rochelle, Cousin Miranda, and so many others made me feel seen and safe in a suburb that rarely featured people who understood my upbringing, let alone accepted it. Margo, Jocelyn, Amanda (all the staff at the homeless shelter), Don F., Mr. Pointe, Profé, Officer Giant-White-Man… Too many names to list, yet each playing a vital role in keeping me afloat. I love and thank all of y'all. So what's the lesson? Actually, I've got a few:

1. No matter where we find ourselves, humans have a remarkable way of making a dollar out of fifteen cents. Strong spirits aren't easily broken, and where there's a will, there's a way. We've proven that time and time

again. If you're feeling lost or low right now, I promise you— circumstances will improve. This world is better with you in it. The darkest point of any day is midnight, and it literally only lasts a minute. After that, the sun begins to rise. Hold on. Change is on the horizon. Better is coming and you deserve to see and experience it for yourself.

2. Living in a bubble isn't an excuse for not knowing or doing better. Yes, it's true, we don't know what we don't know until we're forced to confront it, but we can't use that as a cop-out for chosen ignorance or self-limiting views. Bubbles pop. Always. To pretend otherwise is to plan for failure. Get outside your comfort zone, try something new, learn something different, and don't wait until life slows you down to start regretting the things you didn't explore when you had the chance. The world is bigger than any one perspective. Go see it.

3. Spend time with your loved ones while you still can. Tomorrow isn't promised, and the last thing any of us wants is to be stuck playing the "Should've, Would've, Could've" game when it's already too late. You've been meaning to tell someone how you feel? Now's a good time. Been thinking about owning your role in a conflict? Pick up the phone and do it. Been putting off visiting someone who's sick or shut-in? Don't wait. Even if the person on the other end doesn't appreciate your affection or return the gesture, you'll feel a weight lifted from your shoulders— the weight of guilt, shame,

resentment, anger… all the heavy stuff—, and once it's gone, it's a lot easier to stand tall.

Majors and Misses

Grace Through Soul

MAJORS AND MISSES

THIS PART OF THE book is all about assumptions, how we hear, think, and feel based on desired outcomes, and the (sometimes uncanny, sometimes cruel) link between expectations and reality. What you're about to experience is packed with teenage bravado, semi-toxic levels of masculinity, a hint of narcissism, and a splash of delusion topped off with the image of me playing into those characteristics, rocking jeans three sizes too big, a white t-shirt so long it technically qualified as a dress, and a headband worn every step of the way (except for on the basketball court, ironically). You've been warned.

From the moment I started believing in myself academically (somewhere between Chalmers and high school graduation), I'd consistently earned pretty solid marks in school. As a result, colleges from all over the country began sending me brochures, invitations, and recruiting materials with their best pitches for why I should consider enrolling into their programs by the end of my sophomore year. As a poor kid with low self-esteem, battered by years of bullying in elementary school, I was beyond flattered to find out that dozens of colleges actually wanted me. "Teron, your new home awaits," "Teron, your tomorrow starts today," "Teron, see yourself here," "Teron, the only thing missing is…

you." Every week, two or three letters would show up in my mailbox, and as you might expect from a teenager starved for validation, I read every single one. Top to bottom. Start to finish.

For the first time in my life, I felt like I mattered. Like I had value. As if all the crap I'd been through somehow meant something or that all the hardship had a purpose and led me to this point. And since someone had taken the time to write and send me a letter, I figured I at least owed it to them to read it. How naïve of me. It wasn't until much later that I learned colleges purchase the names of students who take certain exams and spam them with semi-personalized recruitment material based on enrollment goals. I wasn't special. I was a metric. A data point. Still, it felt nice.

One day, near the end of junior year, a college admissions counselor set up shop just outside our high school cafeteria, hoping to catch the attention of students heading to lunch. I'd love to say I was drawn to her table because I wanted to learn more about the university she represented, but I can't. Truth is, I thought she was cute, and since my hormones had flooded me with a wildly misplaced sense of confidence, I figured I'd slide over with my seventeen-year-old charm and work some magic. This, of course, was before I realized seventeen-year-olds have no charm to begin with. In fact, if there were a credit score for teenage charisma, I'd have been in the negatives, unable to borrow a library book without at least two cosigners. After tuning in and out of my daydreams and her pitch, I snapped back just in time to hear her say, "Well, it was nice talking to you, Ron. Here, take my card. If you ever want to visit, give me a call and we'll set something up."

Quick sidebar: I spent all of high school going by "Ron." Most teachers and classmates found it too difficult to pronounce my real name, so instead of correcting them, I gave in and convinced myself I preferred the shortcut. It was a small but telling compromise, marking the start of my long journey with code-switching and changing pieces of myself to be more palatable to those around me. More on that later. But during that pivotal pre-graduation conversation with Mr. Pointe, he encouraged me to surround myself with peers who shared similar lived experiences and to show up as my authentic self. He reminded me that my mother gave me my name for a reason and pushed me to begin thinking about the boy I was and the man I'd like to become. Okay, back to our regularly scheduled programming.

So, there I was, standing there with her business card in hand, thinking to myself, *Oh, I see what's happening. My game is impeccable. My vibe? Irresistible. The magic is working on this college re-cute-er* (sorry, had to)... *Not only did she just ask me out, but she also gave me her number!* That's what I took away from her gestures of leaving me with a business card and inviting me to visit campus. I told y'all, high school Teron was a little dense, and that might be putting it kindly.

Anyway, I scheduled a visit and the campus was gorgeous, complete with perfectly manicured grass, top-notch sports facilities, a prime location in the heart of the city, and most importantly, my fine admissions counselor who, in my gravely mistaken mind, was mere moments away from melting like a puddle for me. We walked around campus for about an hour as she pointed out buildings and hangout spots, but I didn't catch a single word she said since my mind and wildly unchecked imagination were in a completely different place. At the end of the tour she gave me a T-shirt, voucher for lunch in the cafeteria, and encouragement to grab a bite to eat. Her treat. *What!?* I marveled to myself. *Not only did she ask me out and gave me her number, now she's buying me lunch and giving me gifts, too!? Oh man, I got this college thing on lock.* Yeah... I had no idea every student who visited received a shirt, by "her treat," she really meant "this'll come out of the admissions office's discretionary fund, and most critically, she was married and completely uninterested in me. Apparently teenage hormone factories aren't equipped to spot wedding rings or the obvious signs someone is just doing their job. Again, dense.

Fast forward through all the boring application stuff: I was admitted into the college, received a scholarship letter I mistakenly interpreted as stating everything would be covered, got help from Profé to figure out how to pay the enrollment fees, and digested one last reminder from Mr. Pointe to be myself and develop a presence within my new home's Black community. I jumped onto a social media platform that was only available to folks with college email addresses and began my search. If you had an abundance of melanin and were anywhere in the university's network, you were getting a friend request from me. "Hey, I'm new to campus and looking to meet cool people. Can we connect?" Whether it was a shot in the dark, a widely cast net, or a desperate cry for attention—call it what you will—it worked. Before I'd even set foot on campus, I'd made a couple dozen "friends," gone on a few dates, and (at least in my head) was well on my way to running that joint. I was gonna be the man.

SILKY SMOOTH

A YOUNG LADY NAMED Dee accepted my friend request that June, just a few months before college started. We'd spend hours talking online about absolutely nothing, counting down the days until classes began. She was already a sophomore, so she knew the lay of the land, and more importantly—I cannot stress this enough— she liked me. Like, genuinely liked me. Now, I didn't let that get in the way of my untethered, whore-ish expectations for what college might have in store, but I took note, for the record. Every day we found new ways to keep the conversation going, starting with a note on social media in the morning, shifting over to instant messenger around 10:00 a.m., and continuing to chat there until roughly 4:00 p.m. We'd take a short break for dinner before moving to T9 texting (if you don't know, ask your mom), but had to be strategic since neither of us had unlimited messaging and weren't willing to risk a surprise ten-cent charge per text. No worries, we reserved the option to pick things up after 9:00 p.m., when our free nights and weekend minutes kicked in. Anyone born before 1997 knows exactly what I'm talking about.

I was grateful for Dee's friendship and appreciated her kindness, but I wasn't looking for a relationship. I'd always assumed college was the time to let my proverbial hair down and sow my wild oats. Somehow the shy, self-conscious kid I'd always been had transformed overnight into a girl-crazy risk-taker, already having gone on two dates with two different girls and scored the phone number of a third all in the span of a month. Sure, for some of the real players out there, those numbers might seem laughable, but for me it felt like I was having a rookie-of-the-year type season, with no plans of fewer aggressive at-bats. Radical testosterone, am I right?

Options

Summer orientation kicked off on July 21 and wrapped up the following afternoon. In theory, I would show up to take my placement exams for Spanish, Math, and English, grab my student ID, check out my dorm, and head back home. But that plan was far too basic for me, so while all the other soon-to-be freshmen were off doing responsible things like buying books and meeting with financial aid to make sure they wouldn't get booted for unpaid balances, I had bigger priorities: girlfriend hunting.

Today's kids would call it "shooting your shot." Well, call me Mr. Buckets because every time I touched the ball, I was pulling up from half court. Now, terrible analogies aside, what I'm about to describe next is important, like, plot-advancing-important. You already know how Dee and I connected online, but I want you to catch every detail as I walk you through the moment I met my future wife in person for the very first time. Lock in— it's crazy. Some might even say *imagined*.

I stepped out of my Spanish placement exam and caught the eye of a cutie sitting on a bench across the quad, casually eating french fries. I strolled over with the confidence of every '90s R&B male artist who sang, cleavage-exposed-through-an-un-buttoned-silk-shirt, in the rain. I got within a few feet, snapped my fingers, looked away (just to let her know I didn't need *her*, but I knew she wanted *me*), licked my lips and said: "Ay, girl... yeah you. I choose you. Hurry up and come with me before I turn my attention to someone else. Don't miss out on the opportunity of your (but certainly not my) lifetime. You're welcome." Unable to resist my steely confidence, suave demeanor, and six-dollar bottle of Heat Wave body spray, I knew I had her. Just like that, Dee was mine.

Now, there are folks out there who would swear this version of events is wildly inaccurate. They might say I've conveniently forgotten key details or exaggerated others but, since I'm the one writing the book, their opinions don't matter. Wanna set the record straight? Open a blank document and have at it. Until then, that's my story and I'm sticking to it. On a completely unrelated note, if anyone has a couch I can crash on for a few nights... let me know.

Meeting someone for the first time is hard. I'd like to think I'm a decent guy, easy to talk to, and generally good-natured but, even though Dee and I had been texting all summer, connecting in person was... different. There was no response delay or extra moment to step away and compose a clever reply. This was real-time. Face to face. The Thunderdome. Still, I think I must've done at least halfway alright because five years later she agreed to be my forever-person. But, man, hindsight is 20/20.

About three weeks after orientation, I asked Dee out for an official and proper date. We hit up a little pizza shop near her house, watched a cheesy teen romance movie where the couple finds love through the power of dance (insert vomiting emoji), before heading back to campus to meet up with some of her friends. I think she wanted a second opinion or backup in case I turned out to be a total weirdo, which was fair given my recollection of how eighteen-year-old Teron tended to show up. I tried to play it cool but couldn't keep up the charade as my regular, goofy, over-the-top, non-debonair self clawed its way into the driver seat. Lucky for me, her friends didn't seem to mind, granting me their seal of approval by the end of the evening.

Around 10:00 p.m., Dee called me. No greeting. No small talk. Just a question: "So... what are we?" Now, had she asked anything else, I probably would've had four clever answers at the ready, but this one caught me completely off guard. I froze. With no charisma, wit, or smooth deflection, I blurted out the first response that came to mind; the one I thought might buy me a little time: "I don't know. What do *you* think we are?" Boom. Nailed it. Tossed the ball back into her court. Off the hook (or so I thought). "I don't know," she said. "*You* tell *me*." Damn it. Well played, Dee. Very well played. We volleyed back and forth like that for a few minutes before I finally caved and asked if she wanted to be my girlfriend. She said yes, and having gotten the interaction she was looking for, promptly hung up the phone without so much as a "goodnight" or "talk to ya tomorrow."

At the time, I didn't think much of how that conversation played out, but I've now come to recognize that instance as the first in a long line of "questions" Dee would ask that aren't *ac-*

tually questions but instead are carefully disguised and sharply pointed *statements* with only one acceptable response. The writing was on the wall from the beginning and I, once again, completely missed it. Third time's a charm— dense.

Trophy Boyfriend

Dee was one of those kids who always had something going on. From the moment she could walk, her parents had her enrolled in a rotating schedule of sports, camps, volunteer gigs, you name it. So it wasn't all that surprising that by the time I met her, she was a full-time college student majoring in applied mathematics with a secondary concentration in engineering, and a two-sport varsity athlete. Volleyball in the fall, basketball in the winter. Me? Yeah, no. Not my lane. I wanted all the free time I could get. The college we attended had invited me to "try out" for the football team (I use that term loosely, because while it was technically a collegiate sport, the coach didn't cut anyone. If you showed up and opted to wear the pads, you were on the team). He even invited all the prospects to a game to soak in the atmosphere. You know, the kind of cinematic moment where you're brought to the fifty-yard line and asked to imagine the crowd cheering your name.

And while the vibe in the stadium was electric, there was one tiny problem— the team was terrible. The scoreboard at halftime read 35–7, which isn't exactly the dream scenario for a recruitment pitch. I looked at the kid sitting next to me and said, "Yeah… I think I'll stick to intramural sports." That was dumb. I should've suited up. Should've at least tried. But instead of believing I could help change things, I took the easy way out, and now, decades past my prime and having traded in shoulder pads for heated ones that help with joint stiffness, every now and again I catch myself wondering *What if?*

Even without playing, though, I managed to build a name for myself in the athletic world. I was the "trophy boyfriend." If Dee had a game, I was there. Rain, snow, sleet, finals week; I was in the stands, front row, hyping her up. A few of us fans got so into it I'm pretty sure opposing teams started factoring us into their pre-game preparations, which was fair because we had scouting reports of our own. Full rosters with notes on player tendencies, weaknesses, vulnerabilities, and rudimentary psychological profiles. Dee had her sport, but this was *my* varsity season.

Take the girl who always dribbled exactly three times before passing. We'd chant, "Dribble… dribble… dribble… PASS!" right as she released the ball, living rent-free in her head. Or the one who couldn't make a free throw to save her life, we started keeping count aloud, just to be helpful. Or the player who only dribbled with her right hand. We weren't mean, we were educational. "Hey, there's this whole other direction. Try it sometime. It might cut your turnovers in half." Then there was the player we encouraged to consider alternate hobbies. "Book-reading! Rock-collecting! People-watching! Underwater basket weaving! Video-gaming!" We were actually ahead of our time on that last one.

But Katie… oh, poor, sweet, innocent, and unsuspecting Katie. She was the left hitter on her volleyball team and having a rough night with the added misfortune of my crew and me being in the stands. Miss after miss. Block after block. She became our main character. "Katie's on our payroll and earning it tonight." "Katie, that was your ball." "Katie, your team is trying; why aren't you?" "Katie, this L is yours alone." At one point, the ref stopped the match and issued a warning after our heckling started taking a visible toll. Honestly, I'm surprised he didn't toss us out. If I were in his position, Lord knows I would've.

After the match, a man—I'm assuming it was Katie's father—met her at the gym doors, pulled her in for a comforting hug, and held her tightly as she sobbed into his chest. The look on his face as I walked by revealed the inner thoughts he'd tried to hide away: the motivation was already there, so now all he needed was means, opportunity, and a plan to dispose of the body. If he had his way, I'm sure I would've been memorialized on a t-shirt complete with start and expiration dates. If Karma is real, I need to start preparing now, because if/when my own kids hit the court, I just know I'm getting it all back, plus interest.

Not all my fanboy antics were shameful. In fact, I renewed my certification as an A+ boyfriend at a basketball game on Valentine's Day in one of the most lovingly nausea-inducing ways imaginable. Playing at home, Dee was matched up against the biggest player they had and absolutely holding her own. I remember being dialed in and admiring her heart while thinking I couldn't have been prouder. Toward the end of the game, a few friends and I snuck into the hallway behind the team's locker room, lining it with flowers, balloons, candy, and teddy bears. Right at the door, I placed a beat-up old shoe and a box of chocolate kisses, along with a note that read: "I'd walk a thousand miles for one of your sweet kisses." I know, I know... your boy's got game. No need to tell me.

Of course, while I was away, I missed something important. Dee had dislocated her finger and needed to get it popped back in on the sideline before returning to the game like a warrior. After the final horn made the victory official, she and her team celebrated at halfcourt before running back toward the locker room and straight into the surprise I'd set up. A pause. A gasp. A shriek. One of the players read the note out loud, which was followed by an audible "Awwwwww" that swept through the hallway and back onto the court. It was such an astonishingly beautiful moment that Dee's former coach still brings it up whenever we see her. Dee was mortified. I was floating as high as could be. And isn't that really what Valentine's Day is all about? One person showering the other with a grand romantic gesture while the other tries to downplay embarrassment and ignore the physical pain of their L-shaped pinky?

Worlds Collide

My two younger sisters have always seen me as less of a brother and more like a father, or at the very least, cool uncle. I can't and won't take credit for raising them, but we went through hell and high water together. Death and loss. Terrible boyfriends. Homelessness. Parental addiction. And that one time my sister got a scrape on her leg and left a small smear of blood on the toilet seat, which I hysterically mistook for her getting her first period. I panicked, grabbed every absorbent cloth in the apartment, and called my mom in full-blown crisis mode, sobbing into the phone, begging her to come home, and telling her I was in way over my head. We'd been through it all and then some.

When Dee entered the picture, it wasn't exactly shocking that they hated her at first. Not because of who she was or how she acted, but because of what she represented. If I was their father-figure, Dee was the stepmom sent to ship them off to boarding school, never to be heard from again. In their eyes, she was a DEFCON-1 threat; someone who would steal me away or make me choose, and deep down, they feared I'd already made my decision.

They weren't entirely wrong. I *did* leave home, get married, and move in with her, but I didn't do so at their expense. Instead, like most families, we found a new rhythm. A balance that worked for us. I looked for opportunities to stay connected, hosting sleepovers at our place, playing video games, and cracking jokes into the early hours like we used to in the good old days while Dee made a deliberate effort to earn their trust, spending one-on-one time with each sister to build a bridge and ease their worry. And over time, they softened, slowly letting their guards down and beginning to see her not as a threat, but as someone who genuinely loved me *and* them. Today, if I'm being honest, I'm pretty sure they like her more than they like me. Who am I kidding? Of course they do. Traitors.

On the other side of the coin, there came a day when it was my turn to meet Dee's family, and I was terrified. I'd never met a girlfriend's parents before and my imagination ran wild with every worst-case scenario I could think of. By the time the day arrived I'd convinced myself that her dad had plans to strap me to a polygraph, waterboard me in the basement, or break a few international laws just to figure out who I really was and what my intentions might be. I was her first boyfriend and had seen how these things usually played out on the big screens. You know how Hollywood tends to exaggerate, right? Yeah, they didn't this time…

I rang the bell while trying to stop the audible clacking of my knees and control the liberal "giving" nature of my bladder. Dee answered, but before I could greet her, a booming voice echoed from upstairs. "Hey, is that him? Is this the guy?" her father bellowed. He came down the stairs so aggressively, I almost lied and said, "No. Just here doing door-to-door vacuum sales," but opted to tell the truth since I didn't have with me the appliances necessary for him to buy my cover identity. I stepped inside and tried to introduce myself, but before I could get a word out, he threatened, "I've got a urine test for you in the basement. Meet me downstairs." Most guys probably would've been rattled, but not me. I'd been preparing for this moment my whole life. I mean, I was—and still am—the squarest square of all squares. If the other squares held an election to decide who among them should lead, I'd come in second… because even they'd think I was too square. "You got it!" I said. "Let's do this!" I was ready. Never drank, never smoked, never touched anything I couldn't pronounce. Her dad laughed, looked over at Dee, and said, "That's the right answer. Come on in."

Her family was… impressive. And confusing. Frankly, I thought they might be sociopathic liars. Her dad was a high-ranking juvenile probation officer. Her mom was a successful chemist. Together, with Dee and her younger brother, they were the kind of structured, high-functioning Black family I'd only ever seen in sitcoms from the '90s (and certainly hadn't known first-hand).

They didn't just tolerate each other, fight for the hell of it, or weaponize old grievances to do current harm. Instead, they did weird stuff like genuinely enjoying each other's company, cracking loving inside jokes, and sitting around the dinner table to eat a meal. Together. At the same time. Without the TV on to drown out the sound of people they lived with. A bunch of wackos if you ask me.

For the longest, I thought it was all an act. Too scripted. Too perfect. I'll give you an example: the very first time I had dinner with them, Dee's little brother turned to me and said, "Can you pass the rolls and biscuits?" The rolls and biscuits. What was this: seventeenth century France? Was he also going to ask for his top hat and monocle? Maybe suggest we gather around the grand piano for a tune while sipping Earl Grey in front of the fire?

If you thought it stopped with their core four, think again. They loved opening their home. Summer BBQ? Come on over. Graduation? Let's celebrate here. Christmas music and story time while baking cookies from scratch? Of course. And after only a year of knowing me, they even extended those invitations to my sisters and mom. I remember thinking, *Where the hell did y'all come from?* To me, they were the odd, nutcase exceptions to the rule, and though I was slow to adjust, they never treated me like I didn't belong. Once I earned their trust (and believe me, I worked for it), they welcomed me as one of their own.

Still, it was becoming clearer by the day that Dee and I were raised in two very different worlds, and my skepticism or disbelief was a manifestation of how I coped with the embarrassment I carried about my own upbringing. The shame of feeling like I didn't measure up, I guess. During spring break, for example,

Dee and her family flew to Detroit to visit her grandparents, taking in her dad's childhood haunts and doing a little sightseeing along the way. Me? I scraped together enough for a twenty-dollar student-discount bus ticket to Chicago. When I returned, I found out my mom had pawned my video-game console to buy drugs. Can you spot the differences?

ME AND THE BOYS

I N COLLEGE, I HAD no shortage of acquaintances and friends. But a few relationships were forged in fire, hardship, loyalty, and just the right amount of age-appropriate immaturity and have stood the test of time. While I'm my mother's only son, I swear I found brothers from other mothers.

Take Rafael. We met in high school and immediately bonded over being Chicago transplants trying to stay sane in a state, Minnesota, that felt way too slow, quiet, and polite for our liking. When Dee's dad first met him, he joked that Raf was the kind of friend every guy needed— someone who'd show up no matter what, no questions asked. And that might be the most accurate description I've ever heard. I could've been getting jumped by twelve trained fighters or alphabetizing soup cans, if I pinged him, Raf would've already been pulling up before the call ended. To this day, he's one of the most consistently reliable people in my life, and I probably don't tell him enough how much he means to me. This is my reminder. Love you, bro.

Then there were the brothers I met in college. James 1.0 wasn't just the most jacked and fastest guy on the track team, he was also one of the kindest people I'd ever met. Funny, quick-witted, grounded in who he was and what he believed.

Then there was Phil. Deep-voiced, old-souled, and quiet, but when he spoke, we shut up and listened. Sometimes his jokes were so layered I'd start laughing two minutes after the punchline, still trying to put it together. Malik was the wise upperclassman who had a way of steering us in the right direction without making us feel like we were being micromanaged. Patient, present, always ready to show up if anyone needed anything. James 2.0 was technically Dee's little brother, but I'm pretty sure I stole him from her. I was clearly the cooler older sibling, and if Dee has a different version of events, she can write her own book (and get out of my comments section with those hateful remarks). James kept things light. When I began spiraling about the future, he kept me grounded in the present. And then there was White Mike. The melanin-challenged brother I didn't know I needed but loved having. Usually the only two guys in our social work classes, he and I grew together from goofy kids to justice-minded professionals trying to serve others with humility and heart. Mike had the rare ability to make you laugh one minute and then hit you with some deep insight the next. But, equally important, if any of us ever got in trouble, we'd need someone to talk to the police. White-Mike was our delegate.

Reggie

When I think back on the most meaningful, impactful, and long-lasting relationships from college, Reggie easily takes the silver medal, right behind Dee (sorry, bro, but she's looking over my shoulder as I type this, and I know that you know that I know that you know exactly where you stand). But seriously, Reggie and I go back like rocking chairs. We met during summer orientation and kicked things off with a brief rivalry over our mutual interest in a few of the same girls, but after it became painfully obvious that neither of us was the ladies' man we thought we were, our friendship took root. We roomed together our freshman and sophomore years, co-rented an apartment after graduation, stood as best men in each other's weddings, and became godfathers to each other's children. When I say we were bonded, I mean B-O-N-D-E-D. I've always felt indebted to Reggie, not just for the loyalty and laughs, but because—whether he knows it or not—he literally saved me on more than one occasion.

First, he kept me enrolled in college. Remember that scholarship letter I mentioned? The one that made it sound like my entire education would be covered? Yeah... it wasn't. Not even close. Being broke afforded me access to federal and state aid, sure, but those funds didn't increase with the cost of attendance. Each year tuition and fees went up, but my aid didn't budge. I was heading straight for a financial cliff and didn't even know it. Uncle Mike helped as much as he could, but I was still short nearly ten thousand dollars each year just to cover housing and meals. Enter Reggie.

He decided to apply to be a resident advisor sophomore year and casually floated the idea to me. I didn't see myself as the type who could lead a floor full of students, but if it was good enough for Reggie, maybe it could be good enough for me too. You know the old saying, "Monkey see, monkey follow friend blindly because he himself doesn't yet know how to form original thoughts," that's it, right?

Not knowing how competitive the process would be, I figured I'd give it the old college try (is that where the phrase comes from?) and see what happens. I was scared. The application process was intense: scenario-based questions, roleplaying, panel interviews. Tough. The idea of telling my personal story and still getting rejected? Terrifying. But somehow we both made it. Reggie got placed on a floor with incoming freshmen while I was assigned to upperclassmen. The role came with a programming stipend, the freedom to run our own communities, and serendipitously covered the ten-thousand-dollar room and board shortfall I was headed toward. Talk about doing it scared and landing on your feet.

But Reggie's biggest save? That one involved Dee. The summer between my freshman and sophomore years, I went back to Chicago to spend time with Uncle Mike, and while I'd made the trip before, this time was different. I was a college student now and couldn't wait to be back to soak in the praise of friends, family, and neighbors who'd watched me grow up. Every "We're so proud of you," "Your grandma would be smiling right now," and "Don't forget about us when you make it big," filled the insecure spaces in my soul with fuel.

Uncle Mike and I hopped from house to house as we caught up with (and absorbed admiration from) friends of his that I barely remembered but apparently knew way back when I was "thiiiiiis big," before capping off our tour at the home of one of his closest and most respected buddies. A man I admired greatly, trusted deeply, and never dared to question. We sat in the backyard for hours talking about everything, though my responses tended to be shorter than what my educational background would've suggested. He asked how school was going, "Good." How are your grades? "Good." How's your mom? Also, "Good." Then he asked if I was seeing anyone. That's when I lit up. I went on and on about Dee, how lucky I was to have found her, and how she supported me without judgment and helped shoulder my emotional baggage like a pro. When I finally stopped talking, I caught a glimpse of the proud ear-to-ear smile he was sporting as he casually nodded along, congratulating me on finding a good partner, and without missing a beat, following up with, "...and who else?"

Wait, what? Who else? I was confused. Was there supposed to be someone else? Wasn't I supposed to be faithful? Isn't that the whole point? "Well," he said, "you sound like you really like this girl, but how can you know she's the right one if you haven't tried out anyone else?" At first it felt ridiculous, but the way he said it—the confidence, the certainty—it got in my head. He made it sound like common sense. Like I was missing out by not exploring other options. "I guess I don't know..." I muttered while slipping into an existential crisis. This was someone who had guided me through challenges in the past and had earned the reputation of being wise and thoughtful. How could he be wrong now? I got back to campus and told Reggie I thought I needed to break up with Dee. "I just don't know if she's the one," I told him. Confused and understandably caught off guard, Reggie rejected the premise.

He had seen how compatible we were, and convinced I was making a mistake, didn't mince words as he called out my stupidity and irrationality. He tried logic. I wasn't persuaded. He appealed to my spiritual side. I shrugged. He even tried physically blocking the door to stop me from leaving. *Can't stand there forever*, I thought. Eventually, he made one last plea. "Okay," he bargained, "if I can't change your mind, can you at least pray on it and decide tomorrow?" At that point in my life I'd started drifting from organized religion, but still believed in a higher power, so I agreed. We fasted, prayed, talked, and by the next morning, I realized maybe—just maybe— that advice from Uncle Mike's friend wasn't universally true, which was all the evidence I needed to walk away from it.

And Reggie? He probably doesn't even remember that conversation. He was just being a good friend. No accolades. No credit. No idea how he changed the entire course of my life. So, if you admire the relationship Dee and I have today or if you see us and think, "That's what love looks like," you've got Reggie, in part, to thank. But before you go nominating him for sainthood, know this: we also got into our fair share of trouble. I won't completely incriminate us in the court of public opinion, but let's just say we made a few dumb, wildly ill-contemplated decisions that carried consequences to match. Beyond the typical college stuff like staying up too late playing video games or skipping the occasional class to sleep in, but decidedly shy of anything that'd land us in a prison cell. Somewhere right in the middle, I guess.

Like the 4:00 a.m. gas station run for hot dogs that had clearly been rotating on the grill since the dinner rush ten hours earlier, followed by the inevitable phone call from separate bathrooms confirming that, yes, we were both violently and incessantly "pouring gravy" out of our bodies and questioning life decisions. Or the time we started an underground fight club in the dorm basement. No gloves, just wool mittens from the campus bookstore, which didn't soften a single punch. One kid took a hit so hard he had to come up with multiple stories to explain the boulder-sized lump on his face. And who could forget "Mattress Wars," where we lined up on opposite ends of the hallway, handed each combatant a twin mattress, and had them sprint toward each other full speed to see who would remain standing after impact? Or my personal favorite, that math lecture where the professor tried explaining the difference between the "A" and "B" sets of data when Reggie asked—with the straightest face anyone could have ever managed—whether he was familiar with the "Dip Set," fighting to hold back laughter at the professor's confusion (hip hop heads know what he did there). We were clowns, and graciously recollecting our antics, I thank God camera phones weren't what they are today. Love you, Reggie.

Like I said, I was lucky. Blessed. Fortunate. I didn't drink, party or use drugs like the movies prophesied, but instead went to class, worked on-campus jobs, played video games, spent time with Dee, and kicked it with the boys. Honestly, the term "friends" falls well short of what they were to me but, oddly enough, "family" doesn't measure up either. Our connection goes beyond any cliché or arbitrary label I can think of, so I won't try to name it. I'll just let it be what it is and let it keep growing into whatever it's meant to become. One thing's for sure: I love those guys more than they'll ever know.

ACADEMICALLY SPEAKING

I DON'T REALLY HAVE much to write home about when it comes to my "scholarly" experience in college. For what it's worth, higher education actually came pretty easy to me. We established in the introduction that I've never been a good reader, but I was an excellent listener, top-tier summarizer, and elite-level BS artist. I had to be since it took me at least three times longer to read and comprehend a single page than it did most of my classmates, and with multiple professors assigning dozens of pages each week, I had to figure something out if I wanted to survive.

This was before the days of AI, so I had to rely on the next best thing: learning how to sound smart without really saying anything new. My method? Skim a few random sentences from each section, note the bolded headers, and build a framework for the chapter. Then, in class, I'd wait for two or three students to speak, mentally connect their thoughts to the handful of lines I'd glanced at the night before, and fill in the rest with common sense. Jackpot. I'd chime in with something like, "Yeah, I agree with Emily and David to a degree, but I'd also offer that blah blah blah." Honestly, it didn't even matter what came next. Gold. Every time. I got so good at "the add-on" that I could flip into autopilot and still land the plane. Hell, by the time I reached graduate school, I'd turned it into a game.

One of my closest friends, Shara, and I would compete to see who could win over the professors first. Spoiler alert: it was always gonna be me. Not because I was smarter— Shara was brilliant, thoughtful, and deeply grounded—but because I was cunningly competitive and lazy beyond belief. I was determined to do as little as possible while still pulling the best outcomes. Shara, to her credit, didn't make it easy. She was real in every sense of the word: authentic, sharp, worldly, grounded. But she was also easy to mess with, and when I really wanted to push her buttons, I'd sit back and let her offer some beautifully con-structed, insightful comment—something profound that clearly impressed the room—only to raise my hand and say the exact same thing a few moments later. Word for word with slightly different intonation and inflection.

"Wow, Teron. That's a really interesting perspective. One I hadn't considered before," the professor would remark as Shara's face predictably twisted into a snarl. Jaw clenched. Bright red. I'd look past her death stare like I didn't notice, an-noyingly basking in the praise thrusted upon me but owed to her. I'd satirically weaponized my male privilege to win the bat-tles, and to this day, we still find time and space to laugh about it.

LESSONS LEARNED PART 3

B Y ALL ACCOUNTS, MY then-girlfriend and now-wife and I should have broken up, and I'm not just talking about the Reggie situation. Years later, Dee finally admitted that she'd once considered ending things herself, months before I returned from Chicago with my way-too-easily-influenced "maybe I need to see other people" nonsense. Turns out, my mom had asked her parents for money to "help pay rent," which in our world, was code for "fund the latest drug run." Believing they were helping me avoid homelessness and wanting to spare their daughter the emotional weight of seeing me go through that again, they obliged. And when Dee found out....let's just say I had some damage control to do. Her justifiable frustrations were rooted in the audacity of my mother's manipulative actions, but my response to her confiding in me inflamed the situation ten-fold as I appeared to be less-than-appropriately outraged by what had happened. In truth, it wasn't apathy, it was shame. And since I was too busy trying to mask the embarrassment, it came off as unbothered or indifferent. Thank God for the better angels of Dee's nature and the benevolent voices from within that convinced her not to give up on this charity case too quickly.

For me, college was never just about higher education. It

was a metaphor; a battleground between what was *supposed* to happen and what actually did. Not knowing how to properly read a scholarship letter and choosing a school I couldn't afford should have been the nail in the coffin. But it wasn't. Instead, I chased down the additional financial support needed to get by while scraping together a few ounces of self-worth and finding brothers and sisters I'll have for life. I was convinced college would be a non-stop party, full of romantic entanglements and too many partners to count. Then Dee showed up and slowed me all the way down, teaching me what patience and part-nership were supposed to look like and effectively turning an aspiring ho' into a husband. Academically, I was the kid who needed ten minutes to read a page, only to realize I'd zoned out halfway through and would have to start over. What should've been a crushing blow actually forced me to find and lean into my strengths—observation, intuition, connection—and used them to navigate around the things that once made me feel small. I graduated with a 3.7 grade point average (twice: undergrad and grad school), earned leadership awards, recognitions, and began to piece together the man I was destined to become. At graduation, Dee's grandfather (Black, old-school, proud, and set in his ways) had called me "one of those smart Negroes," and shared how impressed he was with her and me even though neither of us had jobs lined up and no idea where we were headed.

We dreaded the thought of moving back in with our parents because in our eyes it suggested we'd somehow failed ourselves and them, but retrospectively assessing what could have been, we realized just how misguided we were. Free advice: if you have a safe and stable home to return to, somewhere that affords you the ability to save money, breathe, and build your foundation along the way, do it. Swallow your pride and do it.

Having a plan is helpful and maybe even necessary, but so is being nimble and tapping into the ability to pivot, improvise, and "play a little jazz." You know what I mean, right? It's great to hit every note on the sheet, but sometimes you have to go off-script and scat. That's why we explode with excitement when busted plays turn into thirty-yard gains or why we scream the ad-libs louder than the actual chorus. So to all my Type A people (those who need the I's dotted and T's crossed), it's ok to not have all the answers. I promise you'll find them when the time is right. And to my Type B folks: remember that, while improvisation is helpful in a pinch, playing a little chess might serve you well in the long run. But either way and no matter the characteristic, the smartest bet you can place is on yourself. Don't let anyone tell you differently.

Lastly, to the older folks reading this: please let the young people live. At some point we all start thinking we've been around long enough to "know a thing or two about a thing or two," (and maybe we have), but we can't keep robbing the next generation of the same trial, error, and failures that served to shape us. They're going to make dumb choices, think they've got it all figured out, and reluctantly ask for your help peeling themselves from the ground when they inevitably find out they don't. Be not worried, they'll one day realize that with increased age usually comes greater humility and a broadened awareness of how much *we* have yet to learn, which doesn't make them unteachable. It makes them human. We can't crush their curiosity with our caution. Can't shut down their ambition just because it sounds unfamiliar or unrealistic. I almost lost my wife because an older man convinced me I was wrong for not cheating on her when I "had the chance." And while that advice was clearly trash, I'm sure someone once gave him the same speech, and he thought he was doing right by me in passing it down. And I know some of y'all are probably thinking, "Well that advice was extreme." True. But I bet the young folks we criticize today look at *our* advice and think the exact same thing.

Sometimes I wonder if we keep regurgitating flawed wisdom not because we still believe in it, but because we're afraid that questioning it would dishonor the people who raised us. Or maybe we're ashamed that we didn't push back when we felt it in our souls to do so, but instead blindly yielded to tradition. Maybe we're just now realizing the cost of that silence. Regardless, we owe it to ourselves and the next wave of leaders to evolve our thinking, examine what we've been taught, make room at the table for new perspectives and consider, just for a moment, the possibility that perhaps they know something we don't.

The difference between medicine and poison is dosage. Two ibuprofens will ease your headache. Thirty will make sure you never feel pain again... ever. Let's all reconsider our outputs of confidence, stubbornness, and forced expectations. It might save us or someone we love from a little unnecessary heartache.

Okay. Stepping down off the soapbox.

Vulnerable Strength

Grace Through Soul

Vulnerable Strength

H OW DO YOU DETERMINE if you're ready? Serious question. I'm not trying to be rhetorical or abstract, I'm genuinely curious about how you decided you were ready for, well, anything. Can you ever really know? Sure, you can *think*, but is that enough when you're making decisions with lifelong implications or permanent consequences? And, zooming out for a second, what about the choices you make that won't just affect you, but also the people around you? The ones you love, welcomed into your sphere, or have looked out for you. How do you know you're ready to go down a path that might forever change their lives, or worse, cause them harm or irreparable damage?

Between graduating from college and hitting my thirties, the universe somehow managed to cram decades-worth of experiences into just a few short years. It felt like I was making life-changing decisions every other day and at times. The same line of questioning I just threw at you almost paralyzed me. Not because I was indecisive, but because I was afraid. Afraid of what I stood to lose. What *we* stood to lose.

Now, I know some of y'all are thinking, "Teron, that's a terrible way to look at it. How can you grow if you don't take chances? You're stuck in a deficit mindset and that's not healthy." Cool.

I appreciate the feedback and I won't necessarily disagree. But before you lecture me to death about the upside of taking chances or remind me that living in fear isn't really living, remember this: for people who know what it's like to ice skate uphill, sometimes the instinct to dig in and stand still rather than risk sliding all the way back to the bottom, overrides ambition in the name of self-preservation.

My anxiety wasn't rooted in hysteria or helplessness. Not at all. More than anything, it was grounded in knowing what it's like to come from struggle, hustle for your next meal, fight just to exist, or always needing to be one step ahead because you know what might happen if you ever let your guard down. This wasn't some theoretical exercise for me. It was real. And while I understood that life doesn't offer money-back guarantees, I couldn't shake the worry that one wrong decision might cost me everything I'd worked so hard to gain.

I didn't want to go back. I wasn't going back.

Nine-to-Five

A FTER GRADUATING FROM COLLEGE, I continued working my on-campus job through the following August, interning for the summer orientation program and helping the next group of leaders welcome incoming freshmen to the university. My boss, "Terri," was legitimately one of the best humans I've ever known. She was this magnificently strong woman—both magnetically and unapologetically so—who'd clearly been through hell and high water. That pain only seemed to deepen her commitment to advocacy, justice, and compassion. From where I sat, she used her power and privilege to shape the next generation of leaders, helping us be a little less self-centered and obtuse, and a lot more mindful of the needs and experiences of others.

But don't get it twisted, Terri was tough. She kicked my butt on more than one occasion when I wasn't living up to the potential she saw in me, but she also knew how to break me down and build me back up. Like that one time she noticed a few of us were monopolizing conversations in our leadership meetings, so she flipped the script and required the quieter—and usually more thoughtful—folks to speak first. It pushed them to find their voices and taught the rest of us that maybe we didn't need to verbalize every single thought that crossed our minds. I later confessed to her that sitting quietly when I had so much to say felt like torture. But the lesson stuck: you'll almost always learn something if you occasionally practice the ancient art of shutting the hell up and activating those weird little holes on the side of your head.

Terri didn't have biological children of her own, but she mothered hundreds, maybe thousands of us. She expanded our emotional intelligence, sharpened our social and cultural awareness, and gave us the courage to use our time, talent, and position to improve the lives of others. And while I might sometimes feel tempted to retreat from that call, if I ever did, I know Terri would hunt me down, reintroduce boot to bottom, and get me back on track. Ugh. Love you, Terri.

Window Shopping

I applied for a few dozen positions but couldn't find my groove. I was eager to start my career but kept running into dead ends. Not for lack of trying, I just couldn't land the plane. I went out for a school counseling job, for example, and quickly realized I was completely unqualified and unprepared. Hell, I'd only gotten the interview because a mentor knew the hiring manager and put in a good word for me. He got my foot in the door but that's about as far as I made it into the building.

Thinking my lived experience might give me an edge, I later applied for a case manager role at a homeless shelter within a massive, seven-story building that served dozens of families. I thought I'd be able to tap into some of the empathy and grit I'd developed during my own recent experience with that challenge, but as I entered the building I immediately felt the immense pressure of what can only be described as "a crossing guard tasked with safely guiding hundreds of people over six lanes of highway traffic." Terrified. *All these people are going to count on me?* My legs trembled as I sheepishly approached the receptionist, who, almost without acknowledging my presence, pointed to the elevator and told me to head up to the fifth floor. As I walked toward the mechanical double doors of destiny, he called out to one of the younger female residents for assistance.

"Kiki, make sure he gets up to the fifth floor. He's here for the interview."

"Uh huh. I'ma make sure he gets to exactly where he needs to be. Trust," Kiki playfully shouted back.

Now, remember how mind-numbingly slow I was in high school? Half a decade later, not much had changed. I thought nothing of her response, but the receptionist made a point to sternly warn, "Hey, man, don't let her get you into no trouble." I brushed it off and got into the elevator with Kiki trailing behind. She stepped to the keypad and casually pressed six. In my mind I thought, *I could've sworn he said five*, but I didn't want to offend her offer to chaperone, so I yielded to what I assumed was her better knowledge.

We got off on the sixth floor and walked down the hall toward a door. Kiki used a key that'd been in her pocket to open it, which really should've been my second or third red flag. Why would a resident have the key to a room where interviews take place? C'mon, Teron; you're supposed to be smarter than that. It wasn't until she flirtatiously invited me inside—before entering, I clocked what appeared to be her personal belongings— that I finally pieced it together. My internal alarms, though long over-due for new batteries, went off. I backed away, thanked her for her interest (because that's what you're supposed to do when declining a sexual advance, right?), and briskly walked back to the elevator, heart pounding. I was in over my head and so taken aback by the interaction that I never even interviewed. I got into my car and just left.

After several more unsuccessful attempts, I was encouraged to apply for one of two admissions counselor positions at my alma mater. In that role, I'd be responsible for guiding high school students through the enrollment process, from the first letter in the mail to their first college class. But I wasn't holding my breath. There were hundreds of applicants, and I was con-vinced it would end like the rest: a polite email letting me know they'd gone with another candidate.

But this time was different. I was in my element. I'd spent the last four years building a brand, forming relationships, and gathering experiences that could now help me seal the deal. I'd rehearsed endlessly for those bland and predictable interview prompts: "Tell us about a time when…" and "How do you handle conflict with a colleague who…?" I was ready. I fielded every question with the ease and confidence of a tennis player serving for match point on the heels of three straight aces. Afterwards, I was charged with delivering a five-minute mock presentation to the current admissions staff, who would fire off prewritten questions designed to stump me. Nerve-wracking, but I was locked in. And then came the question I'd been waiting for: "Why do you want this job?"

My mind had a million routes it could take. I could talk about how special and proud I felt getting those "personalized" letters back in high school. I could tell them how my admissions counselor sealed the deal for me (while omitting the more awkward and libido-driven origins of my interest). I could explain how I misread the scholarship letter, made one of the worst financial decisions of my life, and somehow turned it into one of the best. Or maybe I'd mention how, aside from the semi-annual acts of hate—like when someone wrote "all niggers must die" on the sidewalk, threatened my friends simply for being Black on campus, or scrawled graphic homophobic graffiti on whiteboards in permanent marker— those four years had been some of the most empowering of my life. I'd broken a cycle of poverty, found lifelong friends, and met the woman I hoped would someday say "yes" to being my forever-person. Or maybe I'd talk about how this role would let me be a resource to all the students who were just like me, trying to figure out their next steps in a world that seemed hell-bent on knowing, "So what are you doing after high school?"

Unable to choose, I went with all of the above, and the interview committee ate it up. Was it my light-hearted demeanor? My deeply personal story and desire to protect students from making poorly informed decisions? Or maybe it was the two-page letter the Dean of Students wrote to the VP of Enrollment, urging her to give me a shot because she felt I reflected the university's mission and had the skills to match. I didn't really care as long as I got the job.

Collegiate Concierge

From the start, I knew the role was important. Not because I had some sudden moment of enlightenment where I realized I'd be helping to guide hundreds of students into their next chapter. And certainly not because of some inflated internal sense of pride or superiority. No, I knew it was important because it was drilled into me from the start. On my second day in the office, the vice president sat me down and said, "Teron, I need you to understand the magnitude of your job. This team isn't just responsible for bringing in the next class of students; we generate the revenue that keeps the doors open and the lights on. We come in early, stay late, work weekends and through holiday breaks. We have fun, but we take this work seriously. When you do your job well, everyone's happy. But when you don't, someone loses theirs."

She'd given this terrifying, pressure-packed speech to every young admissions counselor for the past two decades, setting the tone with stakes that felt nearly life or death. And reflecting on it now, I sarcastically wonder why she felt the need to "inspire" us in such a doomsday fashion. Could it have been because, even though we were responsible for over eighty percent of the university's tens of millions in annual revenue, our starting salaries barely cracked thirty-thousand dollars? Hmm...

Regardless, it worked. Everyone on staff bought in. We were in the office by 7:30 a.m. sharp because "if the phone rings at 8:00 a.m., we need to be ready." The workday technically ended at 4:30 p.m., but no one dared leave before 5:45 p.m. Her office was right next to the exit, and the old creaky floorboards ensured every departure was announced with full body shame acoustics. You couldn't sneak out if you tried. For all intents and purposes, we were indoctrinated hostages, trapped in a scenario where time spent in seats was the measuring stick of our commit-ment. Clocking out at your scheduled time? That just meant you weren't working hard enough.

Some coworkers figured out how to game the system. They'd knock out their real work by 4:00 p.m., close their doors, and binge-watch shows until 6:00 p.m. Me? I hadn't yet learned to work smarter, so instead, I worked unnecessarily harder. I used PTO to catch up on emails, vacation days to review applica-tions, and even committed the mental crime of feeling guilty if I wasn't constantly producing. Want to know the worst part? The coworkers who finessed the system consistently delivered better results than I did. Part of that had to do with the stu-dents I supported— most came from historically marginalized backgrounds, required more hands-on guidance, were denied at higher rates, and had fewer financial resources. But I didn't see it that way at the time. From my point of view, my stu-dents' challenges were a direct result of my perceived short-comings. I assumed I was a worse employee, which spiraled into a one-sided love affair with perfectionism, self-doubt, irrational fear, and a desperate urge to code-switch, shapeshifting into whatever I thought others needed me to be.

But it wasn't all doom and gloom. Despite some unwise habits, my time in admissions had more ups than downs. As a Black man with my background, for example, I was assigned to support prospective students from inner-city communities. These students were brilliant, strong-willed, and resourceful.

Many were first-generation students trying to break generational cycles, with some using bits of my story as fuel to propel
themselves when the road ahead seemed fraught with hazards.
And though they may not know it, *they* were helping *me* remain
centered as I slowly crept into a world that looked and felt polar
opposite to the one I'd been born into. They reminded me of
who I was, where I came from, why I was here, and where I
was going. So, while my role may have been small in the grand
scheme, for some of the people I supported, it meant everything, and I didn't take that responsibility lightly.

To my students, I was a guide through an unnecessarily complicated process. Over time, I gained the trust of communities,
teachers, advisors, parents and colleagues, earning the privilege
to lead scholarship selection and distribution to prospective
students who personified our university's mission and vision. I
had this whole act where I'd visit a student's school, request they
be pulled from class to "discuss an issue" with their admissions
or financial aid status. I'd lead with, "Unfortunately, there was
a mix-up with your scholarship and we'll have to revoke it,"
drawing it out just long enough for their body language to signal
they were spiraling, then I'd hand over the real envelope with
their award letter inside. They'd skim every word, but you could
always see the moment their eyes locked onto that one golden
line: "This scholarship will cover your full tuition." That was it.
That was all they needed to read. And reread. And read again.
Then came the light in their eyes, joy, disbelief, and finally, tears.

I was eventually asked to lead admissions for a two-year program serving students with high financial need. It was a brilliant
setup: four semesters of debt-free general education with full

academic support like laptops, bus cards, meals, textbooks, tutors, you name it. We knew that if we removed the obstacles that shouldn't have been there in the first place, these students could thrive. Socially. Academically. Professionally. Groundbreaking insight, huh?

Though I knew I was doing meaningful and system-changing work, therein was the problem. That combination of intense onboarding pressure and my deep-rooted desire to see my students succeed was what blurred the line between personal and professional for me. In each student I saw something exceptional and unrelenting. Young scholars who came from so little and had to go toe to toe with classmates whose families could drop tens of thousands on a vacation without batting an eye. Privileged students with elite academic prep, expansive familial and professional networks, and far less generational trauma to shoulder. And my students still showed up, competed, and shined. I'll forever be in awe of the spirits they carried and will always hold them near to my heart. Some might even say, like a proud dad.

First, Comes Love...

To absolutely no one's surprise, I knew I was going to propose to Dee as soon as I had enough money to buy her what I believed was a proper engagement ring. But since I had no clue what I was doing, I ended up settling for one that fit my budget and wasn't exactly the awe-inducing diamond I'd originally imagined. To this day, I wish I'd broken the bank and bought her that gaudy, over-the-top rock I thought she deserved but couldn't afford. Any time she senses my regret, Dee firmly reminds me that while she loves every symbol of my commitment, she also appreciates that we didn't have to choose between ring payments and groceries. Though I value her recentering, her grace only intensifies my inner spiral→ *Don't you love her? Well, show her. I hope I got a nice one. Maybe... but not good enough. She's pretending to like it to protect your feelings. Man, she must really love you→* And then we're back at the top of the loop again.

Permission, Please

I bought the ring in late July after graduation, but decided to sit on it until August for a few reasons. First: Dee and I, for all our progressive thinking, both agreed I should ask her father for his blessing (I know, I know... feel free to chastise me later). Second:

August 18 was our four-year anniversary, which meant I could propose on a day that was already sentimental and create the full-circle moment she'd come to expect from me by then. And third: I needed time. Not just to prepare my pitch to her dad, but to convince myself I was worthy of asking Dee to spend her life with me. I had some repressed fears—deep-seated stuff—about perpetuating cycles of hurt. I worried I might one day repeat the emotionally, physically, or financially abusive behaviors I'd witnessed growing up, creating yet another generation of broken households.

I called Dee's dad and asked him to meet for dinner. We'd never had a one-on-one before, so I'm sure the request raised at least one eyebrow. We made small talk over appetizers while I tried to steady my heartbeat, which by that point was surely visible through the three layers of sweat-drenched clothing I'd worn to hide the flood pouring from my armpits. Pro tip: don't believe anything those deodorant commercials tell you. I applied no fewer than fifteen swipes and still managed to rival Niagara Falls. Eventually I worked up the courage to deliver the speech I'd practiced since the day I slapped my credit card down to buy that modest little pebble, though I don't recall having as many prepubescent voice cracks during rehearsal.

"Dee and I have been through a lot over the last four years. She's supported me through family issues and helped me grow from a goofy, childish, and immature young boy into a goofy and slightly less childish and immature young man. And while I don't think I'll ever fully believe I deserve her, I want to spend every waking moment trying to prove that I do. If you'll allow me, I'd like to ask for your daughter's hand in marriage."

There it was. The point of no return. I laid all my cards on the table and waited in silence while he digested my words. "You know," he said, "I actually thought you were asking to meet so you could tell me you were dumping my daughter." I chuckled, but he didn't. "No, I'm serious," he continued. "I actually have a baseball bat in the trunk of my car. I was ready to bash your head in."

Well... damn, I thought, *I guess I should take that as a compliment? In his eyes, I was such a good fit for his daughter that breaking up with her would be cause for a bloody beatdown. Should I say thank you?*

He sighed in relief, flashed a half-smile in my direction, and began to share that he'd always like me because he saw bits of himself in my reflection—something about my grit and refusal to quit, but honestly, I wasn't paying attention. I couldn't. I was so overwhelmed by the moment that you could have paraded a line of elephants past me and I wouldn't have even noticed. Regardless of the reason, I snapped back to reality just in the nick of time to register that he'd given his approval. And just like that, I was holding a soap-opera-level green light to move forward with the biggest ask of my life. I couldn't contain my excitement as I jumped up and hugged Dee's dad…hard. Gawkers looked on with confusion, but I paid them no mind. I joyously sat back down, asked if he'd like to see the ring, but before he could even answer I had already slid the box across the table. He opened it and smiled from ear to ear. I couldn't tell if he was happy about the future he'd envisioned for his daughter playing out before his eyes, or smiling like, "Aww, look at that itty bitty wittle diamond." Either way, I was counting it as a win.

Just then, our waitress walked over. "Hey guys! I saw that big hug; what are we celebrating today?" She glanced down and saw him holding the ring box with a huge grin. "Oh my gosh! Congratulations, you guys! This is amazing! You make such a cute couple!" Dee's dad and I had a choice: correct her... or ride it out, knowing there was a decent chance they'd comp the meal if they thought we'd chosen their establishment to publicly declare our love for each other. I'll let your imagination decide which route you think we took.

Do me the Honor?

August 18 rolled around, and the big day was here. To avoid any awkward silences or accidental slips, instead of driving together, I asked Dee to meet me at her favorite casual Italian spot. As I got out of the car, I was convinced the ring box was bulging so noticeably from my pocket that she'd see it instantly. I gave her a big hug, a kiss on the cheek, and held her hand as we walked inside, where we were seated immediately. Suspiciously, immediately— Too immediately. Almost like they knew what I was planning and wanted to make sure their restaurant got a flattering review in the inevitable memoir I'd someday write about the moment.

The waitress brought over a couple glasses of water and asked if we needed anything else. I perked up, "Actually, yes. Could you take our picture? It's our four-year anniversary." She smiled and happily obliged as I handed her my digital camera (remember those?) and let her do her thing. Snap. "How's this one?" She handed it back for review.

"Hmm... I'm sorry. Can you take another one? I want it to be perfect." She tried again. Snap. "Okay, how about this one?" I grimaced. "No, I don't know what it is, but it's just not coming out right. Can we try one more? Sorry to be a bother." By now, Dee was visibly embarrassed. She apologized on my behalf, shot me a look that said, "Dude, it's just a picture," and told the server we'd make do with what we had. But by then, it was too late. The waitress, still holding the camera, glanced at what was happening just over Dee's shoulder and immediately understood the assignment. Without warning, she started snapping photo after photo. Confused, Dee turned to me and got the clarity she was looking for.

There I was. Shakily trying to balance on one knee, ring in hand, staring up at her with every ounce of faith and love I could muster. The annoyance in her face disappeared, replaced by joy and disbelief. She burst into tears, hugged me tighter than she ever had before, and screamed "Yes!" loud enough for the entire restaurant to hear. The crowd went wild. Total strangers clapped and celebrated with us as if they'd been rooting for this moment all along. Just like that, we were engaged. Having barely touched our food and too hyped to eat, we rushed to Dee's parents' house to share the good news and begin crafting the world's most elaborate announcement spreadsheet. One column for in-person conversations. Another for phone calls. A third for texts and emails. And a final one for social media. Leave it to Dee to systematize love.

My Wife And Kids

W E SPENT THE NEXT year entirely focused on planning our wedding and navigating all the logistical and political landmines that came with it: choosing a venue, booking the caterer and photographer, locking in a DJ, and creating the longest and most arbitrary guest list imaginable. You know the one, filled with people we felt obligated to invite but secretly desired only about a third would show up.

And while I wish I had crazy stories about everything going wrong or tales of bachelor party escapades that ended in blood oaths and overnight jail stays, I don't. Auntie Patti, our wedding planner, handled all the heavy lifting. By the time she was done, our only worries revolved around Reggie losing the ring or Noelle's (one of Dee's bridesmaids and most loyal friends from high school) mascara running from tears of joy. I mean, sure, there was the off chance that someone might awkwardly stand up to profess their true feelings for either of us during the "if anyone should object to this union..." section, but the likelihood was pretty low. So, aside from the standard family drama at the reception about who owed whom money from 1973, or which cousin was *actually* at fault for losing that game of Spades in the mid '80s, there wasn't much to manage.

And the pre-wedding festivities? Just as tame as the rest. The guys and I went to an arcade, played laser tag, and figured out how to hit that one machine just right to get unlimited gummy candies. Meanwhile, Dee and her ladies hung out at the rec center, fashioned toilet paper wedding dresses, and voted on who wore it best.

Seriously, there's not much to write home about. For the first time in my life I didn't feel anxious or fearful about what was coming. I guess that's what happens when you find your person; they make even the scariest stuff feel routine (but don't tell her I said that. She'd never let me hear the end of it).

I Do; Do You?

Ask anyone who's ever been married, and they'll tell you: your wedding day is one of the fastest-paced experiences of your life. Doesn't matter if you show up at the venue at 6:00 a.m. or 3:00 p.m., it feels like you're already late and have maybe fifteen minutes before the show starts. Even still, our day went off without any major hiccups. Well... mostly. Sure, the pastor mispronounced Dee's name (DeJurnett'... Dee-Shuh-Nay). And yeah, he missed his cue and skipped one of the songs our cousin Robbie and the pianist had spent a whole week rehearsing. And of course, my mom wore a white dress... because she figured she was just as important as the bride and thought everyone should—and would—know. Oh, and we didn't eat a single bite of dinner because we were bombarded with congratulations from well-wishers before we could ever lift a fork. Eventually we left the reception early and grabbed fast food on the way home.

But none of it mattered. Because at the end of the day...blah blah blah...[insert sappy line about soulmates and feeling complete]. Sorry. I've already given her enough compliments in this section. Moving on.

Even with everything going so beautifully, life wasted no time reminding me that you can't outrun your past. A couple of months after the wedding, Dee got a terrifying call from Grandma Nancy. Apparently, someone had called and left a message saying I'd been in a terrible car accident and urgently needed her help to get in touch with my dad. The timing was awful as I'd left home just an hour earlier to give a presentation to a group of high school students, which made the story seem frighteningly plausible.

And this was back when sharing your phone's location wasn't nearly as sophisticated as it is now. According to Dee's device, my phone (and body...) appeared to be floating in a lake roughly forty minutes from home. She rounded up her parents, jumped in the car, and sped off to try and find me. When they arrived at the lake and saw my car wasn't there, she had a moment of relief, but that feeling didn't last as she now had to wrestle with a new and equally daunting question: *where the heck is he!?* Then it hit her. Thanks to our trusty family calendar (kept meticulously up to date under threat of court-martial), she realized where I'd gone. The high school.

Dee and her parents burst through the auditorium doors to find me at center stage, giving what could only be described as the most engaging presentation about financial aid and application deadlines those students had ever witnessed (though, to be fair, the bar was low). Confused but ever the showman,

I carried on without missing a beat. Later, Dee filled me in on the panic she'd experienced. Though it took a couple days to unravel, we eventually learned the truth: some goons in Chicago were trying to smoke out my dad and they thought using me as bait might get his attention. Six hours away. Three hundred miles from home. Nearly a decade removed from that life and still, it had its hooks in me.

Getting Ready

Gangland movie plotlines aside, life was going great. Eighteen months into marriage and Dee and I were doing better than ever. That's not to say we didn't have our share of growing pains and learning moments, but I'd finally helped her understand that if she could just accept the fact that I was always right and completely without flaw while she was overwhelmingly to blame for every conflict, we'd get along just fine.

No, seriously. Things were good. So, like many newlyweds in our shoes, we started talking about expanding our team. On the surface I was cool and composed. But inside? I was spiraling. This was the same Teron who didn't have much to draw from in the way of positive fatherhood models, and now Dee expected me to become one? Sure, I'd seen Uncle Mike, Mr. Strader (more about him in a moment), and Dee's dad show up in father-like ways, but none of them were *my* dad. And at the time, that still held a lot of weight in my mind. I couldn't see that chosen fathers could be just as impactful—maybe even more so—as biological ones. I was too jaded and had convinced myself that parenting behaviors were inherited. And if that were true, then

I was certain I'd fail. Spectacularly.

Thank God for my baby sisters. While I was lost in a pit of anxiety and self-doubt, they pulled me out, inch by inch. Normally, I was the deliverer of stern talks and life lessons, but this time I was the one on the hot seat. Over the course of a few months they gently—and not-so-gently—reassured me that I was as prepared as any future dad could be, and had receipts to prove it, readily listing off all the things I'd helped them with over the years. Driver's ed, homework, cooking, getting to school on time, college admissions, even paying tuition. They reminded me that no matter what I had going on, I always showed up. Birthdays, breakdowns, and everything in between. I gave them encouragement when they were down, direction when lost, and a metaphoric boot to butt when needed. I'd chased off more than one sketchy friend or romantic interest and even welcomed my sisters into Dee's and my home when our mom kicked them out of her house. So, yeah, while I still had a lot of learning to do, they helped me realize that I'd already cleared the minimum qualifications for the job. Love you, Tameka and Tachena.

But just as I checked one existential crisis off the list, another popped up. Now that I was slightly more confident I wouldn't ruin my future children, I started worrying about character-building. *If I'd grown strong because of my struggle, did that mean our kids (who wouldn't face that same level of hardship) would be weak?* Somehow I took everything good in my life and reframed it as a liability, seeing the stability that Dee and I had created as a hindrance. I searched for irrational reasons not to pursue fatherhood, treating every flimsy argument as rock-solid evidence against it. Then, like the hero at the end of a comic book right as the villain tightens their grip, an unexpected savior swooped in to save the day: social media?

Hoping to get a glimpse of what might lie ahead, I joined an online group for dads. It wasn't perfect (about seventy-five percent of the posts were bitter rants from men complaining about their kids' mothers, calling them spiteful, manipulative, and vengeful), but there were a few gems if I looked in the right places. One lesson, in particular, stuck with me. It was a post from a guy well-known in the group for his hot takes:

"Man, kids today are soft. Cotton candy. Snowflakes. They don't know what it's like to hustle. I fought for everything I had. Every day. And now they're living off the grind I built."

I nodded along as I read, agreeing and believing that he'd captured exactly what I'd been feeling with unimpeachable proof and undeniable passion. He had me convinced, but as is required in the bylaws of S.N.O.O.P. (the fictitious "Social Network Oversight & Online Policy" I made up just now), I scrolled to the comments section with my bucket of popcorn to see if someone would kick the hornets' nest. There were hundreds of likes, dozens of affirming responses, but one tiny counter-narrative tucked three-quarters of the way down the page caught my eye.

Another father simply asked, "My guy... isn't that kinda the point?"

Wait, what? Sir, how dare you completely shatter my entire worldview by calling out that the goal isn't to pass down the trauma or make our kids fight the same uphill battle we had? You mean to tell me that the struggle was supposed to be *ours* and not *theirs* while also arguing that raising children with stability and love is not only acceptable, but necessary? Or that breaking cycles of chaos and poverty is a good thing and raising my future children with love and compassion would actually ensure they'd be more and better equipped to face the world? Whew. With one seven-word comment on a random social media post, a whole new level of understanding opened up to me. I was ready (...ish).

Derrick James and Jordyn Bea

Over the next five years, Dee and I welcomed two littles into our family. Derrick (DJ) joined our crew in the fall of 2013, but I remember the moment we told Dee's parents we were expecting like it was yesterday. Her mom squealed, leaped into our arms with a corny jump-hug, and screamed with pure joy. I'd never seen her so overcome with emotion. Her dad, on the other hand... well, that was a different story. The look on his face said it all even though he tried to hide it. I've always been good at reading body language and his was crystal clear: "You did this to my daughter? I oughta kill you." Funnily enough, he apologized years later, admitting he wished he'd responded differently and rationalized that, if I ever had a daughter of my own, I'd understand. I was tempted to ask, "didn't you think this might happen after we got married?" But I opted, instead, to hold my tongue. I'm goofy and immature, not clinically insane.

When DJ came into our lives, everything changed. I know that's the most unoriginal thing any new parent can say, but clichés are commonly used for a reason; there's truth to them. In a third-person, out of body sort of way, I watched over myself from the delivery room as I held him in my arms thinking,

Wow. I can't believe this little dude is mine, before immediately following with, *No seriously… this lil dude is mine? Like, I can just take him home? No test? No certificate? No user's manual? What happens if he springs a leak? Is there a warranty?* Nope. Nada. Just us. Two people who made a huge, life-altering decision without collecting his insights first.

Over time, DJ began to show his true colors, literally and figuratively. Literally, he was light-skinned. Very light-skinned. Like, borderline translucent. And while he eventually grew into a generously-melanated skin tone, I used to joke with Dee that he resembled the mailman. She never laughed, though. Never found it funny, I guess. Maybe my delivery was off (see, now that's a double pun: delivery… birth… mailman. You get it. Moving on). Figuratively, he was becoming this little human right before my eyes, and I couldn't help but marvel at how impressive I thought him to be. He was bright, emotionally attuned, musical, always dancing and singing while sporting sink hole-deep dimples and a ridiculously infectious laugh that could light up a room. And man, did he love his mama.

For the first couple of years, he wanted nothing to do with me. When Dee left the room he cried, and when he heard her footsteps returning, sprinted toward the door as if to get away from the "mean old man" who was clearly in over his head. Eventually learning that she and I came as a package deal, he began to reluctantly tolerate me as a means to an end. No worries, however; as he grew, so did our relationship. I worked hard to show and not just tell him that he could always come to me with anything (and I mean anything), and I'd be there for him with zero hesitation. Would there sometimes be consequences? Of course. But he'd be loved, no matter what. He's since taken me to task on that promise dozens of times as I've seen him share hard truths and own up to things he was probably ashamed of, waiting to see if I'd be a man of my word. And with every instance, I tried to meet him with the empathy and compassion I'd sworn to extend to him from the day he was old enough to understand.

Can I just say how proud I am of this kid? He's almost everything the world doesn't expect a little Black boy to be: smart, charismatic, caring, giving, and ridiculously clever. He's always smiling, joking, asking how he can help, and passing out hugs. You know how people say that kids raised on love move differently than kids raised on survival? DJ is living proof. He doesn't know it, but he's the one who taught me that affection doesn't have to be earned or transactional, but that sometimes people love you just because they do.

That said, I think we may have created a little too open of a household situation for this dude... DJ would walk into the kitchen early in the morning with a question that required immediate response, often posing it while standing uncomfortably close to my face and half-dressed. Like, bro, I'm cool with you dropping a knock-knock joke every now and again, but could you move your penis at least six inches away from my cereal bowl first? Please and thank you.

Jordyn was a completely different story. She arrived in late winter of 2017, and for the girl-dads out there, you already know how everything changes. You start looking at the world differently, dusting off the workout bench and conducting internet searches for how to lease a military-grade helicopter to hover

over your house for the next twenty-five years. Now before you call me out for being overprotective of my daughter and not my son: yes, you're absolutely right. Guilty as charged. I grew up in a neighborhood where little girls were forced to become little women way too early, and if their partner dipped out when things got real (which happened often) they were left holding the bag alone. I've softened a bit since then, but I still keep eyes in the back of my head and the Pentagon on speed dial.

Luckily, I probably won't need either. Jordyn is the most resolute, assertive, strong-willed, and outspoken little girl I've ever known. She's sharp and loving, confident and kind, having even received an award in kindergarten literally stating as much: "The assertiveness award goes to Jordyn for speaking up, knowing what she does and doesn't like, and standing up for herself and others." She's never once made me doubt whether she'll fly high in a world that might try to clip her wings. Sure, she loves dolls, unicorns, rainbows, and occasionally dreams of adding a purple streak to her hair, but don't get it twisted: she *will* tell you off to your face without flinching.

But here's the thing: Jordyn's not assertive for assertiveness' sake. She simply has bold standards. She expects high character from herself and those around her, doesn't compromise on her values, and refuses to accept anything as truth without evidence. For example: she was enrolled in an extracurricular math and reading program to help stretch her academically, and for two days a week, she attended in-person classes while she worked from her tablet at home the remaining days.

One day she asked, "Dad, why do I have to go in twice a week? It's loud and distracting. I can't focus." I tried to explain, "Well, the teachers need to help you if you get stuck and test you to make sure you're ready to move to the next level." She wasn't having it. "But all the work gets downloaded to my tablet. And the teachers never help me while I'm there because they're with other kids. So, I'm basically doing it all myself, just like I do at home. Can't I just come in for the tests and do the rest from home? It's quieter. Plus, it saves you time and gas."

"Uh… well… see… Mommy and Daddy pay a lot of money and…" I had nothing. Grasping for any straw I could, but finding none, I surrendered to being stumped by a seven-year-old. We emailed the program director, and within the hour, got confirmation that they too would bend to her will, caving to her logically-sound request because they too failed to find a flaw in her intense line of questioning. Girl's tough. So, Jordy-Cakes, if you're reading this, daddy loves your spirit and your strength. But if you could maybe use a little less of it on him, I'd appreciate it.

They say parents are born the same day their children are. And I'm starting to believe those might be the truest words ever spoken.

The Ones Who Came Before

When I think about the parent figures I had throughout my life, one word comes to mind: fortunate. Even during the roughest years, I was lucky to have the parents I did. As you know by now, it wasn't all sunshine and lollipops, but each of them gave me something valuable, something I still carry. My mother, for all her flaws, showed me that parents will do whatever it takes to make ends meet. She taught me that if you want something badly enough, the only thing standing between you and the goal is your will to reach for it. My father? He taught me that when everything else falls short, you roll up your sleeves and get your hands dirty. He showed me how to keep my head on a swivel in hostile territory and to never let outsiders threaten your family's safety.

When my mom moved to Minnesota, she met a man I only ever called "Mr. Strader." Not because I didn't accept him as a father figure—I did—but because I respected him so deeply and had grown so indifferent to the word "dad" that this felt like the most appropriate way to address him. He was patient, loved my mom fiercely, and gave her everything he had (and then some) to make her happy. He was the carpenter stepfather I mentioned back in the intro, and despite showing up late in my life (and in this text), he played a monumental role in shaping the man I'd become. In true woodworking fashion, he taught me that even the most meticulously crafted blueprints sometimes require on-the-spot pivoting when things don't go according to plan, that some bonds take longer to mend than others, and that sometimes you need professional help to navigate the tricky parts. But the core lesson? When something breaks, it doesn't have to stay broken. Let that one simmer.

Dee's parents (Steve and Lori) taught me the power of family structure, and what a healthy one could look like in real time. Lori came from a financially challenged upbringing in St. Paul while Steve came from more stable means in the rough-and-tumble streets of Detroit. And though I don't know much more about their pasts beyond that bit of trivia, here's what I *do* know: ever since they met, the only thing that's mattered to them is the life they've built together for themselves, their kids, and their community. Full disclosure, I might be a little biased. But I think they've done one hell of a job and will say more about their impact later. For now just know, if they ever made trading cards for Parents or Community Members of the Year, I'd scour the internet and pay a ridiculous amount of money for theirs. They'd be worth their weight in gold.

Steve and Lori had spent years building trust, putting in work, and supporting the people around them and it showed, especially in Dee's and my relationship. Sore spot alert: it took five or six years of marriage before Dee would take my advice without first calling her parents to confirm it. It could be something simple. She'd have a headache and I'd say, "Take a couple ibuprofen and rest. You'll feel better soon." But she wouldn't budge until after calling her mom, explaining her symptoms, getting the exact same advice, and then immediately following it. Used to drive me up the wall. Not because she wasn't listening to me—okay, maybe that bothered me a little—but mostly because I didn't have that kind of relationship with my parents, and I guess I was a little jealous. Flash forward to now? I'm the one calling Dee's mom for guidance and casual conversation. Dee loves to joke—begrudgingly—that I've become her mother's favorite child, and since she's known her longer than I have, who am I to argue?

Bad Decisions and Fortunate Breaks

I F YOU'VE EVER BEEN suckered into watching one of those criminally predictable direct-to-TV movies or subscribed to a magazine targeted at teens, tweens, or twenty-somethings, then you probably grew up believing your twenties would be the most exhilarating years of your life. A golden age of freedom, fun and time to make memories, messes, and maybe a few mistakes, because you had a whole decade to recover before adulthood really kicked in. It's not entirely wrong, but it's definitely incomplete. Sure, your twenties come with a bit more freedom and maybe some financial independence, but they also come with high-stakes decisions, silent pressure, and real tests that you can't study for, yet carry very real consequences if you don't practice some level of caution. I, like many of you, wasn't just living my life however I pleased; I was deliberately choosing my partner, inadvertently setting my path, beginning to live into some unspoken promises, and making plenty of mistakes along the way.

Petrified and Stuck

Earlier, I mentioned the unhealthy work habits I adopted right after college, and while I didn't lie, I did leave something out. Deep down, I liked the pressure and structure because it gave me something to push against and strive through. It became a quiet competition where I worked to be the first one in the office every morning and earn the highest (though untracked) satisfaction ratings from students, families, teachers, and communities because I needed them to know I had their backs. I was trying to be the kind of support I wish I'd had growing up, which was only compounded and complicated by my internal desire to gain the approval of bosses and colleagues. I leaned into the pressure, let it validate me, and used it to justify some really unhealthy habits that somewhere along the line, turned into comfort, and later, complacency.

I still remember the first time the admissions committee asked me to sign off on a denial letter. You'd have thought they told me to take the kid out back like a racehorse with a busted leg the way I cycled through every stage of grief before finally signing the paper, shutting my office door, and crying for the rest of the day. In my mind, I'd crushed a student's dream. Never mind that I didn't know who he was or that his GPA barely beat the legal blood alcohol limit. I just knew I had helped close the door to him and that haunted me.

I don't know when or where, but I eventually became a cog in the machine, settling into a system that'd once plagued me but now had become routine. Signing denials became just another item on the checklist. Sure, there were a few students I deeply connected with—ones I advocated for hard—but most of the time, I'd slipped into business-mode and the more efficient I got, the more disconnected I became. I started racing myself. *Yesterday I was done by 2:00 p.m.; let's shoot for 1:00 p.m. today.* I wasn't pushing for excellence anymore, I was angling for early clock-outs. Coasting. In that complacency disguised as productivity, I started questioning my worth, pushing away opportunities, and learning to doubt myself more with each new day.

This may come as a surprise to some of my former colleagues, but before I wrapped up my ten-year tenure (see what I did there?), I'd turned down three different job offers. I'd told myself that my students needed me and that my talents were better utilized and needed within the college but let's be real, I was a chicken. Scared to try something new, to bet on myself and fail, or bet on myself and succeed because then I'd have to accept that I had real potential, and that meant I'd have to chase it. Even when I was offered a promotion to Director, I hedged. Told them I was too busy with family and grad school and asked to be bumped down to Associate Director, which came with less accountability and more support... I thought. In reality, they just gave me all the Director-level responsibilities but cut the pay.

Just writing that makes me cringe. I hate that version of me. Thank God for the people who never stopped pushing.

Everyone Lands

When I started in admissions, I met another counselor named Laurel. We'd have these long, layered conversations about everything wrong with the world and how to fix it as we challenged and learned from each other and our lived experiences. Eventually she left the role, moved on to something else, and like most things in life, we fell out of touch. Then one random day, years later, she called me out of the blue. She was now a VP of Growth Strategy at a fast-moving company and wanted to introduce me to her CEO.

I wasn't expecting anything. I hopped on his calendar for what was supposed to be a thirty-minute call that ended up lasting two hours, and by the end of the week, had a job offer on the table. That role eventually grew into a VP-level position with the salary to match, but I was predictably looking for reasons to say no. I asked Laurel to tell me everything she didn't like about the company. I tried to convince Dee that my schedule wouldn't accommodate such a change. I even made a ridiculously biased pros and cons list that heavily favored staying put. I reached out to my boss' boss, Sal, who at the time was unknowingly serving as my mentor, and asked for his advice. All of them told me the same thing: take the job. Reluctantly, I did. Love you, L. You too, Sal.

About three years later, another friend—Shara—reached out with a new opportunity. You remember Shara, right? The one I used to compete with in grad school (was it really a competition if I always won? We'll let history decide). After the program had ended we became about as close as two people could be. Constant contact, encouragement, and always in each other's corners. If I'm being honest, though, Shara poured way more into my cup than I ever managed to pour into hers. I tried to show up, tried to be there when it counted but the truth is, she made a habit of going out of her way to make sure I was good.

Always.

When she saw an opening for a role that would've been a huge step up for me: more responsibility, higher salary, bigger network, and more influence, she sent it my way. And I said no, reciting some crappy lie about being focused on growing in my current position. The real reason was that I didn't think I was good enough. I did a little recon and saw that more than two hundred people had already applied for the position, and given that fact, knew I didn't stand a chance. Uncharacteristically, Shara didn't push; instead, she asked if I'd be her plus-one at a luncheon the following week. Free food and quality time with a friend? Say less.

When I arrived, she was already working the room, mixing, mingling, and connecting with all the "important people." She spotted me, waved frantically, and called me over. "Hey, Teron, this is Brother B. Brother B, this is Teron; he's the guy I've been telling you about. He's really interested in the open role on your team." Now, I'm usually good at keeping it cool, but inside, I was screaming, *The guy she's been telling you about? Shara! What are you doing!?* I. Was. Livid. Initially with Shara, but after a while I shifted the anger to its rightful owner: me. How many times was I going to wait for someone else to believe in me before I followed suit? Brother B smiled, shook my hand, and encouraged me to apply.

Six weeks, four interview rounds, two work simulations, and one logic and reasoning inventory later, I got the job. Yes, I did the heavy lifting, but it was Shara's unshakable loyalty and belief in me that put the barbell in my hands and reminded me I could carry it. She was like one of those overly encouraging gym trainers who won't let you quit halfway through a rep because they know there's more left in the tank. Love you, Shara.

It's wild, I've always been good at hyping other people up, coaching them to believe in their potential and cheering them on. Using metaphors like:

"Walking while blindfolded is one of the most terrifying experiences a human can have because we're conditioned to crave foresight and the ability to see what lies ahead. Though scary, taking even the tiniest steps forward signifies progress, growth, and development toward a goal. And here's the beauty of it all: when you surround yourself with good people, true accomplices will be there to pick you up if/when you bump into a wall or trip over a curb. Falling down is unavoidable, but as a fighter, getting up is inevitable. Don't be discouraged or afraid of the road ahead simply because it's unlit; that just means it's waiting for *you* to shine."

But when it came to me, I turned into Dr. Low Self-Esteem, PhD in Undervaluing My Own Worth and the country's leading expert in downplaying accomplishments and dismissing praise. Never did I believe the advice I so generously gave to others might apply to myself. Almost as if, when you've trained yourself to see only your deficits, you become masterful at ignoring your surplus.

Lessons Learned Part 4

I OPENED THIS SECTION asking how any of us ever know when we're ready to take that metaphoric leap into uncharted territory. Several thousand words and a few contradictions later, I remain unmoved. You can't. The very concept of "knowing" is so misunderstood that when you really drill down into it, you might start questioning long-held views you've always believed to be fact but more accurately classify as opinion, belief, faith, or strong conviction.

"Teron, didn't you just tell yourself to have more confidence on the previous page? Now you're saying none of us really 'know' anything?" Yep. That's exactly right. It's almost like self-exploration leaves you with more questions than answers and committing to being a lifelong learner might not be as easy as merely saying the words out loud. Weird, right? But for the record, and in my defense, I never promised the roadway of vulnerability and self-discovery would be free of contradictions. The potholes on that path can feel more like sinkholes if you don't navigate with caution or allow for nuance.

It's Not Mutual

Far be it from me to tell anyone who or how to love. Not my place. If someone brings you joy, contentment, security, stability (or whatever other traits you might find desirable in a partner), who am I to judge, stand in the way, or opine? And more importantly, why the heck would you care what some rando off the street thinks about an attraction, orientation, decision, or lifestyle that doesn't even remotely affect them? Live and let love. As long as you both care deeply for each other, share mutual respect, actively work to avoid toxicity or trauma, and agree on give-and-take expectations, I say let it rip. Roll the dice. Fall in head over heels and don't look back. You've got a friend and supporter in me.

It gets trickier, though, when one of you cares more deeply, is ready to say the L-word sooner, or expects something the other person isn't ready, able, or willing to provide. That's when the ground gets primed for conflict. Before long, those little quirks you once found adorable start gnawing at you like a dull, rusty handsaw working its way through an oak tree. Slowly but surely, one of you (usually the one who thinks they're more committed) starts to feel slighted, unappreciated, and bitter. Then it becomes only a matter of time before someone blows up over something small and innocuous like forgetting to wipe out the microwave, skipping their turn to take out the trash, leaving a cabinet door ajar, or putting something in the "wrong" place.

There's a bit of a saving grace, though, if you find yourself in one of those lopsided relationships but aren't quite ready to call it quits. That is accepting the situation for what it is. When you've made peace with the fact that the other person may never share the same depth of feeling that you do, it becomes a little easier to exist in that space without imploding. You can retain hope in the possibility that love might one day show up, but you don't hold your breath. And ultimately, you give yourself the option to walk away if it becomes too much to bear, time hasn't evened things out, or you come across something else that might treat you better.

Plot twist: I'm not talking about romantic partners. You can love your job, but don't expect it to love you back. Let that settle in while you reread this section.

No, I Love **You** More

When Dee and I started dating, the puppy-love stage was as sickeningly sweet as anyone might expect. And when I say sweet, I don't mean "aw, they're so cute together" sweet, I mean "ouch, where did this cavity come from and how much is this root canal going to cost," sweet. I remember dragging out our late-night phone calls by no fewer than ten minutes, arguing over who should hang up first or who loved the other more. Gross, I know. But there was intrigue in the debate. In theory, one of us could (and probably did) love the other a little more. (Spoiler: it was Dee. I mean, how could she not, right?)

And while rehashing that every night sounds exhausting in hindsight, the fun was in knowing that either of us could be right. We don't have that debate as often these days, but don't worry, the kids have slotted in and picked up where we left off. DJ and Jordyn will swear on a stack of Bibles and under oath that they love us more than we love them and there's nothing anyone could say to convince them otherwise.

Here's the thing: they are—and always will be—wrong. Without their consent or consultation, Dee and I decided to bring them into this crazy world not knowing what might be in store, and even before they took their first breaths, knew we'd give up anything and everything in a heartbeat if it meant they'd grow up happy, healthy, and cared for. Not to go super dark on you, but if a crazed horror-movie monster walked in and said, "Teron, it's either you or the kids. Who am I eating?," I wouldn't hesitate:

"Do I have to pick, or are you good with taking both?"

I'm kidding! I'm kidding! Lighten up! Anyone who knows me understands the monster wouldn't even finish the ultimatum before I'd happily raise my hand and march out the door. No regrets, no second thoughts.

Not long ago, I overheard a parent at the grocery store arguing with their kid on the phone as they pleaded, "Why can't you meet us halfway? We give you everything and ask nothing in return. How can you not see how much we do for you and how much we love you?" It broke my heart to hear, yet almost simultaneously, I found myself silently replying, "Because they can't." Maybe they can see what you permit them to, but they can't truly understand what unconditional love feels like until they have to conjure it themselves.

Honestly, I sometimes wonder if it's even reasonable for us parents to get bent out of shape when our kids don't return the love we give them with equal energy. Now, before you jump down my throat, I know there are plenty of parents struggling with this very idea, and that's completely fair and expected. I've just found that, try as they may (or may not), our kids will never grasp the depth of our love for them. Maybe they'll get it if or when they decide to expand their own teams. Until then, the concept's too abstract to comprehend. Put differently: my kids didn't ask to be here, so maybe I should ease up on expecting endless gratitude with zero attitude.

Sad Waffles

After Jordyn was born, Dee and I decided our family was complete, agreeing that we couldn't see a world where we'd add another to the mix. It would be a few years before I'd go in to make it official with the ol' "grip, rip, and snip," but we had a mutual understanding until then. About three weeks after Jordyn arrived, Dee fell ill. I rushed home from work to find her lying on her parents' couch, in so much abdominal pain that she couldn't move. I tried to carry her to the car, but each adjustment made her yelp in agony. The only option left was to call 9-1-1 and pray she could hold on just a little longer.

After what felt like an eternity for the paramedics to arrive on the scene and get her into the ambulance, I immediately hopped into my car and followed closely behind as they sped off. At one point, the driver pulled over, walked up to my window, told me it was illegal to tail them as aggressively as I had been, reassured me they'd get her there safely, and said I should slow down and drive more responsibly. I nodded my head as he spoke, signaling that I understood where he was coming from and put his mind at ease as he returned to the driver's seat before utterly and completely ignoring every word he'd just said. *Really? You're lec-*

turing me on traffic laws while my wife is doubled over in the back of your vehicle? He could've saved us both some time. There was no way I was letting Dee out of my sight. Something about seeing a young mother rushed to the hospital in pain triggered memories from childhood. I couldn't do anything back then, but I'd be damned if I wasn't doing something now.

At the hospital, doctors tried everything they could, but nothing brought relief. Tests, anti-nausea meds, hours of waiting and it all fell short. Even worse, they couldn't figure out what was wrong. Eventually, they discharged her around 4:00 a.m. and instructed me to monitor her for a few days to see if she improved or worsened. I went to her bedside, tapped her shoulder, and explained their "treatment plan." Dee, knowing her body, refused to leave. "I'm not okay. I know I'm not okay. Something's wrong and I'm not getting up." Being the rule-follower I'd grown into, I gently repeated the doctor's orders, but without saying a word, she turned toward me, lovingly caressed my hands as we locked eyes, and violently projectile vomited across the entirety of my midsection. That was all the confirmation anyone needed. The staff scrambled to admit her. My wife, in fact, was not leaving.

Four or five days passed, Dee was getting worse, and the doctors still had no answers. Her bloodwork suggested that, without intervention, things could take a very serious turn. A specialist floated the idea of "exploratory surgery" with the potential removal of a large portion of her intestine, which would require her to wear a colostomy bag for the rest of her life. Best part: there was no guarantee the surgery would even solve the issue, but since it was an elective procedure, they gave us some time to consider. For all the grief I gave Dee about turning to her parents instead of me for advice, I was beyond grateful her mom was with us that week. She knew exactly which questions to ask, what rabbit holes to explore, and how to advocate fiercely for her daughter's care. If I didn't know better, I would've thought she was part of the hospital staff. Nope. Just a concerned mom doing what she had to do.

I had planned to stay at Dee's side until she was well again, but Children and Family Services tended to frown upon parents leaving infants and toddlers unattended. Uninterested in an extended stay in a six-by-eight barred cell after having avoided one up until that point, I went home to relieve a family friend who'd been watching the kids and attempted to step into full-time dad mode. That night, our barely-three-week-old daughter was inconsolable and scream-crying at the top of her lungs. I went through the mental checklist as I worked to diagnose what was wrong but repeatedly came up empty. Diaper? Changed. Bottle? Fed. White noise machine, bouncy chair, lullabies, swaddle? All covered. Nothing helped.

At 4:00 a.m. and thoroughly out of options, I laid her in bed next to me and broke down, desperately and sympathetically staring into her eyes as I began to painfully sob and confess to her: "Jordyn. Daddy loves you with all his heart and soul, and I'm trying my best to be what you need, but I'm weak, a failure, and unable to fix whatever's going on. I'm sorry. I know this is pathetic, and I know it's not your problem, but I'm really struggling right now. I want Mommy to come home too, but until then, this is the best I've got. And I know it's not enough. But I need your help. Please. Help me out. I'm begging you. Please?" I wiped my tears and rocked back and forth, whispering the most depressing mantra known to humankind: "I can't do this by myself. I can't do this by myself."

Jordyn must've taken pity on me, because she finally drifted off to sleep. I followed her lead, both of us collapsing into slumber, not sure which of us had cried more into that shared pool of exhaustion. The next day, Dee's parents called to check in, and when they asked how I slept, I told them everything. No point in lying. For the first time in our marriage, I felt like I'd underperformed in the unspoken role of "man of the house." The societal expectation was that I should be able to handle anything—no breakdowns, no weakness, just sheer willpower, testosterone, motorcycles, and raw dominance. But one of two things had to be true: either my understanding of what it meant to be a strong husband and father was flawed or, more brutally, I wasn't the man I'd expected myself to be. I went with the former. It gave me the sliver of promise I needed to keep trying.

Dee's mom made one phone call, and in the blink of an eye, Auntie Brenda and Kelly (the kids' godmother) appeared at my doorstep, ready to support. They were godsends, with them offering to stay overnight to help with Jordyn and granting me the few precious hours of sleep I desperately needed. I couldn't offer them much in return, and they wouldn't have taken it even if I could. What I did manage, though, was to make them the best breakfast I could whip up with the few scraps of energy and clarity I had left.

Back at the hospital, the doctors finally landed on a diagnosis. During labor, Dee contracted a routine infection. The heavy antibiotics she received afterward killed off both the bad bacteria and the good ones, leaving her gut vulnerable to any germ that wanted to set up shop. And guess who moved in? A life-threatening strain of C. diff colitis. Scary, but treatable and... preventable. While we felt positive about her recovery, we were furious because the delivery doctor should have advised Dee to eat yogurt or take probiotics after coming home to help guard against potential illnesses like this one. That ten-dollar-a-week suggestion could've spared us this entire ordeal. Super cool.

Dee began improving, but I could tell something still wasn't right. This time, it wasn't medical. It was deeper: spiritual, primal, maternal. After a few gentle conversations, Dee finally admitted what was weighing on her: she was heartbroken that she hadn't held Jordyn in almost a week. Her parents reassured her she'd be home soon, but I knew Dee; delayed gratification wouldn't cut it, so I did what any good millennial would and consulted the internet. According to my "research," nearly half of healthy babies under one year have C. diff bacteria in their stool without showing any symptoms. That meant Jordyn was likely safe to be near her mom even though she was battling an infection. So, against the strong (and borderline threatening) objections of her parents, I brought Jordyn to the hospital for Dee to hold. Confirming causation is tough, but the fact she'd improved so quickly after that visit with Jordyn that the doctors declared her well enough to go home the next day has to count for something, right?

Quick public service announcement for anyone willing to listen: you should absolutely trust that your doctors are the foremost experts in administering healthcare. Full stop. Period. No edits. Well... okay, maybe one itty-bitty caveat: make sure they understand culturally concordant care, have a staff that can advise accordingly, or ask for an advocate if you don't already have one. Along the way, Dee and I learned that when we're handed massive amounts of information before a big decision, we're better off slowing down and consulting our BRAIN:

B: What are the **Benefits** or positive outcomes for each option?

R: What are the potential **Risks**?

A: Are there any **Alternatives**?

I: What is your **Intuition** or gut telling you?

N: What happens if we do **Nothing** or just wait?

To this day, Auntie Brenda still talks about those dang waffles I made her all those years ago. She'll tell you that they were the best she's ever had. Hands down. Unmatched. First place with no competition. Real quick: does she not know those waffles came straight out of a box? She had a brother out here feeling like a four-star chef when all I did was add water and oil. That's it. But I'm not gonna tell her and neither should you. Let's not ruin the magic of the moment. The best part? Every time she mentions that breakfast, I'm reminded of something far more important: real strength isn't about powering through or going it alone. It's found in the willingness to be vulnerable, name your needs, and ask for help before you've drowned in bravado, bottling up worries and foolishly taking on more than you can handle. That's what saved me. That's what saved us.

Somebody needs to hear that again.

When It Rains...

Grace Through Soul

WHEN IT RAINS...

T HE HUMAN CONDITION IS interesting. Try as we may, we can't stop ourselves from searching for deeper meaning in the experiences that cross our paths. Heck, this *entire book* has been my attempt to make sense of my past and present, hoping their lessons might help guide my feet toward the future. I suppose it's second nature to want to believe that, when the final chapter is written, everything we've endured (the ups and downs, hardships and heartbreaks, sacrifices and difficult decisions, loves and losses) mattered. That *we* ...mattered.

For anyone who knows me, it's no surprise I think of myself as a bit of an optimist who believes that if we look hard enough and give ourselves, others, and our situations the benefit of the doubt, we can find the silver lining often needed to hold on a little longer, push forward a little harder, or believe that something better is on the horizon. That outlook has carried me through some of my darkest days, but as I've grown older, I've discovered that tempering it with a small dose of realism has helped me hedge my bets and soften the blow of disappointment when it inevitably stops by for a visit. A coping mechanism, I suppose.

Murphy's Law suggests that anything that can go wrong will. Bleak? Sure, but it's also a reminder that when even our most

thoughtful plans encounter setbacks or roadblocks, it isn't necessarily because we failed; sometimes it's just life doing what
life does. The Law of Averages works similarly, asserting that,
given enough time and frequency, outcomes tend to balance
out, which is logic often called on by those of us who have faced
constant struggle and cling to the faith that the coin flip of life
won't perpetually land on tails. It's not all upside, however, because a good number of us use those very same frameworks to
rationalize the degree to which we punish ourselves, especially
those who believe we've reaped more than we've sown and wait
anxiously for the moment it all comes crashing down. Because
God forbid we believe the light in our lives is actually deserved,
earned, or free of some invisible catch.

"All good things must come to an end," "No good deed goes
unpunished," "Wait for the other shoe to drop," "What goes
up, must come down." There's nothing quite like the smell of
my-failure-is-inevitable first thing in the morning to really get the
blood pumping. Layer in a little *what have I done to deserve this?*
or *why me when others are working harder or need it more?* Add
a side of *I don't think I belong here* or *The higher they fly, the
harder they fall*, and you've got yourself a well-balanced breakfast of low self-esteem and imposter syndrome, packed full of
the worst nutrients needed to half-heartedly stumble through
an impossible day.

For years that's how I silently dined. On the outside, folks
saw a happy-go-lucky teddy bear who let problems roll off his
back like a ball down a hill. On the inside, they couldn't see that
same ball careening toward two-way traffic, bound to cause an
accident, or at the very least, force others to stomp the brakes or

adjust their path to avoid a collision. I tucked away my concerns, not wanting to burden others with what I labeled as trivial. After all, I came from a whole lot of "nothing" and had managed to earn a little bit of "something," so what right did I have to feel anxious, worried, or overwhelmed? Beautiful family, comfortable income, stable home, good health. What could I possibly complain about, right? How could I be so insulated by goodwill, love, security, and a host of other blessings most people only dreamed of, yet still feel empty or incomplete? What kind of spoiled, entitled nonsense was I trying to convince myself of?

For anyone who's lived long enough to know better, that way of thinking is foolish. It forces too many assumptions and makes little argumentative sense, gaslighting you into thinking your pain isn't valid because there are "bigger" problems elsewhere, so you diminish the weight of your own burden, which just creates a new, more harmful one. I'm ashamed it took me so long to realize what I was actually carrying—not the petty hang ups I obsessed over, but the real deficits. The biological, emotional, spiritual, social, and psychological ones. The ones that affect our quality of life, make our situations more complicated than they need to be, and invalidate the concept of self-compassion or forgiveness when we fall just short of those impossibly high expectations we set beyond our own reach.

Instead, I did what many kids who clawed their way out of nothingness do: packed all those emotions into a tight little ball and hurled it into the deepest part of my mind, hoping it would sink low enough to go unnoticed by anyone passing through. You know the saying, "hope floats"? Yeah, well apparently so do all those other feelings we try to drown.

Make It Make Sense

I 'VE DRIFTED THROUGH THE vast majority of my adult life feeling like a fraud. I'd earned stellar grades and a bit of a reputation as a leader, role model, and maybe even someone to look up to in certain circles, but something was still off. If you'd asked me, I'd say I fooled everyone into thinking I'd cracked the secret code of life and was living proof that hard work, dedication, perseverance, and a positive attitude were all anyone needed to be successful. And I know I sometimes slightly embellish Dee's admiration for me, but all jokes aside, even she couldn't completely see through the façade I'd thrown up to shield myself and others from the harsh criticisms I held against me.

Members of the community nominated me for leadership awards. Family voiced how proud they were of my accomplishments despite my turbulent beginnings. In-laws welcomed me with open arms because I was seen as a net positive in just about every way. Friends came to me for guidance because I always had a practical spin that helped them address the issue and feel a bit better about themselves. Coworkers brought me their problems because they believed I could help them find resolution. And the kids...Lord, don't even get me started on them. DJ and Jordyn quite literally thought I was the "best dad ever" and took every opportunity to remind me. Everyone (and I mean EVERYONE) who knew me believed I was a standup and admirable guy, so why couldn't I?

Stranger in the Mirror

You ever look at those folks who seem to get along with everyone and wonder how they do it? Like, how can the same person who's ready to argue about which rapper had the better verse on a track buried deep on a trap album effortlessly shift gears and hold their own in a heated debate over the safest mid-sized SUV without skipping a beat? Or how the kid who grew up listening to hardcore gangster rap can turn around and sing Gospel then dabble in punk rock and alternative hits all within a few minutes? Some people might call that person eclectic or eccentric, which are really just socially acceptable versions of *odd*, but for many of us who grew up like I did, that kind of flip flopping between realities comes at a cost most people can't afford.

I'd learned early on that survival meant knowing how to fit in and had the experiences to back it up. Experiences that taught me that those with power sometimes felt threatened by people who represented the narratives they'd been taught to fear. As a Black man, I quickly came to understand that I'd either be seen as part of the communal "bad" or the individual "good" of my people. Hard truth to swallow, but that's the way it's always been. The dominant culture has long held the privilege of being viewed as collectively good, while any bad behavior is chalked up to individual outliers. Meanwhile, people from non-dominant communities are often viewed as collectively deviant, with the highest achievers labeled the "exception" to the rule. That's why no one clutches their purse when a white man walks by, even though statistically they account for the majority of mass shootings and sexual violence. But a Black or Brown person in a hoodie? Folks cross the street, avoid eye contact, and grab ahold of whatever makeshift tool of self-defense their survival instincts can dream up. We've been conditioned to crown the dominant group as harmless but force the rest of us to earn that same benefit of the doubt, all while justifying our prejudice with sayings like "better safe than sorry."

Now, don't get me wrong: I'm not asking for more or less scrutiny for anyone, I'm just calling out the dynamic that exists in systems where power is hoarded and withheld. And even though I love the skin I'm in and wouldn't trade it for anything, I'd be lying if I didn't name the fear that comes with being called "one of the good ones" while also not wanting to be labeled "not one of the good ones." It's a paradox, I know. Contradictory? Definitely. But it's a reality that so many of my spiritual kin wade through every single day.

To cope, I started saying yes to everything. I figured, at the very least, expanding my experiences would make me feel less like an imposter, and at the very most, prove to anyone watching that I was worth the praise. Join the school board? Sure. Be president of a small organization working for access to higher ed? Of course. Serve on two more boards? Why not? Go back to school for an advanced degree at night? Naturally. Become a basketball official, break down game film, ref three or four nights a week, travel hundreds of miles each season? Absolutely. Oh, and don't forget, be a good partner to your wife and a great role model to your kids. Easy, right? Well...

So how do you stay true to who you are while also navigating a world that is often uncomfortable with your authenticity? Dee's dad used to call me a chameleon, but I saw it the way most people in my situation did, code-switching. Shaving off little pieces of myself to avoid being perceived as a threat. I knew how much bass to remove from my voice to sound confident but not intimidating, which phrases to use to make others feel comfortable, and how to nod, make quick eye contact, break it just as fast, and offer the half smile that silently said, *I'm not a threat.* Comforting to some. As for me, I started to lose track of who I really was, puzzled as I tried to make out the image looking back at me from the mirror while futilely attempting to suppress the identity crisis barreling my way. I'd become a master at hiding and could've led a workshop on "safe inauthenticity" if colleges employed professors with that sort of expertise.

During the earlier days of the pandemic, I was working from my makeshift home office when I stepped out after a call and took note of an abnormal look stretched across Dee's face, equal parts concerned and confused. "Who were you talking to?" she asked. "Just someone from work. Why?" I responded. "Why were you talking like that?" she fired back. I didn't get what she meant, so I shrugged it off and went back to work. A few hours later, we had the same exchange, but this time she came with receipts. "Don't talk. Just listen to this," she said, handing me her phone and cueing up a recording. What I heard next was... mortifying. It sounded like something out of a 1950s educational cartoon. "Gee willikers and by golly! That dame must think you're the bee's knees or cat's meow after leading the meeting like that! Ya done good, kid. Real good, see? Keep it up. Okie dokie now, have a super swell day. Alrighty, bye bye."

Okay, maybe I'm exaggerating a little, but not by much. The point is that the guy on that recording didn't sound like me, at all. At least, not the me that Dee, my friends, and community knew, so why had I sanitized myself in that setting? Simple. Because it functioned well. People liked working with that version of me, it got results, and for a long time, that was enough. But after listening as it was played back to me, I couldn't unhear it and decided that day to start showing up more authentically. I vowed to care a little more about being true to the version of Teron that I liked and a little less about how people—who never took the time to know me in the first place—might perceive me because, ultimately, that was *their* problem. Not mine.

Just Don't Look

The insomnia was awful. It started in the fall of 2020 and held me hostage through the winter of 2023 (with a few surprise encores since). I'd lay down around 10:30 p.m., toss and turn until midnight, internally argue about why I couldn't fall asleep and then, somehow without realizing it, look up to see that it was already 7:00 a.m. and time to get the kids ready for school. That was the pattern. Day in and day out, for three straight years.

I tried everything. Meditation. Essential oils. Forcing myself to stay up unreasonably late attempting to exhaust the engine and crash. Nothing worked. I even tried a so-called "hard reset" on my sleep pattern. The plan was to wake up at 7:00 a.m. Saturday morning, go about my day as usual, stay awake through the night, and not sleep again until Sunday at 11:00 p.m., then wake up at 7:00 a.m. Monday, bright eyed and reborn. Forty-something hours without sleep, followed by what was sure to be a restful and restorative slumber. At least, that was the theory.

It didn't work.

Eventually, and only because Dee wore me down, I agreed to see a sleep specialist who asked me to track my habits for a couple weeks and bring back the data. I logged everything: what time I got into bed, how long it took to fall asleep, how many times I woke up, how long I was awake, what time I got out of bed. At the follow-up, the doctor looked over my notes and calmly explained that I only seemed to need about seven hours of sleep each night, but since I had internalized the idea that every adult should get between eight and ten, I was essentially trying to cram a large square peg into a small round hole. "Sleep is like an accordion," he said. "Doesn't matter how far you stretch or compress it; it only has a fixed amount of material." My body only needed seven hours, so laying down at 10:00 p.m. and waking up at 7:00 a.m. just gave me two extra hours to sit there, forcing rest I didn't need.

His advice was straightforward: go to bed at midnight, wake up at the usual time, get up right away, and give it a month. Surprisingly, it worked. Once I got past the weirdness of calling midnight a regular bedtime, it actually helped. For a while. But toward the end of 2023, I started to pay closer attention to what was really going on during those sleepless hours and a theme began to emerge. Sure, part of it was that my body wasn't ready to shut down, but there was also something else at play. Something deeper. Something that couldn't be fixed by pushing back bedtime.

When I left my job in admissions, I wasn't just making a leap of faith, I was opening the door to a whole new level of self-scrutiny without realizing it. I wasn't just walking away from a role I had become comfortably competent at; I was stepping away from fifteen years of familiarity to venture into something unknown. So, every night, as soon as my head hit the pillow, I began spiraling, viciously and unrelentingly questioning if I was cut out for the new line of work, making enough of an impact, or what would happen if I made a mistake. *Would I get fired? Lose my income? Would that leave my family in poverty, the very life I had vowed never to return to?* From there, the worry escalated. In my mind, Dee would eventually divorce me, the kids would be taken away, and I'd end up numbing the pain with drugs and alcohol until I was found motionless in an abandoned building, a flaming barrel of trash flickering beside me as I drifted into oblivion.

Yeah. It got dark. Fast. Every night, new catastrophic scenarios took over, causing my mind to race: *If the house caught fire in the middle of the night, I'd tell Dee to scoop up Jordyn and go out the window (in case the hallway was blocked) while I grabbed DJ. By the time he was safe, I'd be overtaken by smoke and flames, but would die happily knowing that they'd be alright.* When I was feeling especially apocalyptic, I added layers: *What if the tree out front falls and pulls a live electrical wire into our escape path? Or what if I'm home alone with both kids and only have time to save one? How am I supposed to choose? DJ's older and more capable of getting out on his own but choosing Jordyn based on that assumption feels wrong too. You know what: why not just have them sleep with me tonight? Yeah. That's safer. Also, did I turn off the oven?*

BEEP BEEP BEEP. Just like that, it was morning. Time to get up and be a functioning husband, father, employee, and human.

I've always been what some might call vigilant, watching people's hands more than the scenery when in a crowded space while picking up on things that seem off or out of place. Dee and I would be out and about at some boring venue, and while she hummed along to the pop tune playing over the P.A. system, I was counting exits, sizing up threats, noting which tables could be flipped over and used as cover versus those that had been bolted to the floor, and figuring out which person to throat-punch *first* if I'd have even the slightest chance of getting us out of there alive. She was "Mrs. Happy-go-lucky" and had no idea how many times I saved her from imaginary threats of bodily harm. But hey, I wasn't doing it for the praise or recognition. I did it for the…. paranoia?

That level of attentiveness kept me in a constant state of readiness, which is likely why I've been characterized as a good defensive driver, calm under pressure, and a quick thinker when things go sideways. Maybe it traces back to the time in third grade when Patrick cracked me upside my head with a lunch tray after we'd gotten into an argument earlier that day. Or maybe it was my mom drilling into us as kids: "to be aware is to be alive." Whatever the reason, I learned to keep my guard up.

The breaking point came when Dee went out of town for a long weekend, leaving me alone with the kids and parentally fighting for my life. On the final evening of my solo parenting, I found myself attempting to be in two places at once as Jordyn had basketball practice and DJ needed homework support. Thankfully, there was a work area about two hundred feet from the gym that offered DJ a quiet study space while I accompanied Jordyn to the court. I smiled as I watched her begin to walk in her mother's footsteps, wondering what might come if she inherited the entirety of her parents' average height and even a morsel of her father's long-forgotten athleticism. Then it hit me like a sudden rush of worry and anxiety: DJ was alone. *What if someone tries to kidnap him?* I silently questioned as I urgently speed-walked to check on him. Leaving the gym and rounding the corner that I was convinced would eventually become ground zero for the FBI manhunt, I was beyond relieved to find he was still there, intact and not in need of an Amber Alert. Though the worry had passed, I decided I'd sit with him for a bit to ensure the potential predator hadn't coincidentally stepped away just as I happened to check on my guy. But, before I could really settle into any semblance of comfort, the fear washed back in: *Oh no! My baby girl's drink is just sitting on the court unattended. What if someone slipped something into her water bottle while she's not looking?* I full-on sprinted back to the gym, metaphorically broke out my forensic analysis kit, and confirmed her bottle had not, in fact, been tampered with. Then it hit me again. And again. And again. For the next hour, I ping ponged between study area and gym, caught in a loop of protection and panic that I couldn't stop.

Once the kids were asleep, I sat with how irrational my behavior had been, feeling embarrassed, ashamed, and unable to find the courage to tell Dee. *What if she thought I was losing it? What if she took the kids? What if I ended up in that abandoned building after all?* I tried to hold it in for as long as possible, internally arguing that I was sparing her from unnecessary worry when, in truth, I was too afraid to be vulnerable. Once that reality set in, I cracked, breaking down and telling Dee everything I'd been hiding since the day we met. How I'd been feeling like a fraud since college. How I never felt like I deserved the awards, promotions, or praise. How the worry that once haunted me only at night had started creeping into daylight and shaping my behavior.

Just like that, it was out. The toothpaste had been squeezed and there was no putting it back in the tube. I braced for what I thought might come next, recounting stories I'd heard—especially from other Black men—about opening up to a partner only to be met with ridicule, scorn, or a quiet withdrawal of respect. The pressure of that possibility pressed down on me as I waited what felt like hours for her reply. I braced for catastrophic impact, but instead, was met with care and compassion as Dee looked me square in the eyes and returned a lovingly sharp "About time. I knew something was off, but I didn't want to keep bothering you about it. Let's get you some help."

It's funny for a few reasons. First: anyone who knows Dee knows her reaction would be nothing short of supportive. Second: I have a degree in clinical social work, you'd think I'd have practiced what I preached and sought help earlier. Third: the irony isn't lost on me, my irrational worry about how Dee (and others) might react to finding out that this seemingly well put-together guy was struggling with mental health kept me from seeking the help I needed, which cultivated the breeding ground for more anxiety that I couldn't talk about because I worried people would see me as "less than," which created more worry, which led to...You see the cycle? Yeah. Me too.

I won't bore you with the gritty details, but let's just say that after a year, two therapists, a psychiatrist, several hours of intense testing, and a few thousand dollars, I finally had a name for it: Generalized Anxiety Disorder, Attention Deficit and Hyperactivity Disorder, and possibly some underlying Post Traumatic Stress Disorder. The inability to read, comprehend, and retain, which led me to create shortcuts that got me impressive grades without the effort. The anxiety that crept in at the most random and inappropriate times, forcing me into constant doomsday prep. The disbelief that I'd ever really *earned* anything and the even stronger belief that if I had, it would (and probably should) be taken away at any moment. Suddenly, it all made sense.

Writing the word "psychiatrist" still takes a ridiculous amount of strength. There's something about admitting that I needed one that makes me feel vulnerable in ways I didn't know I feared, but mine offered up a course of action that included practical techniques, lifestyle shifts, and medications. I was game for all the exercises and habit changes, but pills? Those terrified me. Being born a "crack baby" and growing up in a family where substance use was no stranger made me wary of putting anything chemical into my body, even if it was a "good" one. It took a while, but eventually I reminded myself that I needed to commit to the healing process. Not just for me, but for Dee, the kids, and the people who counted on me to be steady. I owed it to them to lean into what I was avoiding. I had spent years telling myself I was operating at full capacity when, in reality, I was spinning my wheels in survival mode. So, I made the choice to move forward, even if I was a little apprehensive.

Let me tell you: when I say my eyes were opened, I mean wide open. The impact of the medication was almost immediate and so profound I genuinely questioned if this is how people had been living all along. Not constantly running through mental survival drills for every possible worst case scenario or waiting until the last second to do something, then spiraling because it wasn't perfect. *People actually live like this? You mean to tell me I've been out here white-knuckling my way through life all this time while y'all were out here breathing calmly and finishing things early without panic attacks?* Rude.

Aside from the inevitable grief that came with realizing how different my life might have been had I sought help sooner (another story for another day), I felt amazing. For the first time in recent memory, I believed I could do or be just about anything. To be clear: I still had worries, and I occasionally encountered moments of overthinking and hesitation, but they lived at a more manageable volume that likely landed somewhere within a normal range of concern. And life? Life was good. But of course, as I foreshadowed at the top of the chapter:

"All good things must come to an end." "No good deed goes unpunished." "Wait for the other shoe to drop." "What goes up, must come down."

It Comes In... Sixes?

G RANNY PASSED AWAY IN November of 2002, and my entire world fell apart. The shepherd of the family was gone, and predictably, the flock scattered. Some tried to honor her memory by building a better life, breaking old patterns, or starting over somewhere new, but some unfortunately fell deeper into the cracks. If you fast forward about fifteen years, it would've been easy to label me as one of the lucky ones. My mom had managed to get her footing in Minnesota, my sisters were pursuing college degrees and starting families, and I'd graduated, married my best friend, landed a good job, and become a father. On the outside, everything looked like it had come together, but inside I carried just as much fear of losing it all as I did pride in having built it. I tried to hide my weak points, but Dee knew. She always knew.

Every summer since moving to Minnesota, I made a trip back to Chicago to visit family. After we got married, Dee started tagging along not just to keep me out of trouble, but to uncover more about who I was and how I got to be the man she fell in love with. On arrival, we settled into my usual rhythm of checking in with Grandma Nancy and Grandpa TC, hanging out with Cousin Ebony and her kids, swinging by Aunt Gloria's, schooling Auntie

Rochelle in a few hands of Casino, linking up with Miranda and the boys, driving through my old neighborhood to point out life landmarks with commentary like, "to your left, you'll see the park where I got beat up and had my bike stolen for the first time," and finishing off with a trip to my favorite restaurant to grab Italian beefs, hot dogs, cheese fries, and chocolate cake milkshakes. Pro tip: calories don't count on vacation. I read that somewhere on the internet, so it must be true.

About a month before this particular trip, Dee and a few trusted elders started gently planting seeds, suggesting I reach out to my father in an attempt to reconcile my anger and make peace with the past. Externally, I was adamant: absolutely not. I'd shut that door, locked it tightly, compartmentalized the trauma, and left it in a box far away from my current life. But deep down, I was torn. Something in me whispered that, beyond being necessary for me to heal, I wanted to see him again and potentially patch things up. Even with all the years, all the hurt, all the haunting memories of my mother pleading for him to stop, I was still just a boy who wanted to be around his father.

I got in touch with one of my older sisters, Quita, to track down my father's address, and after a bit of rudimentary stalling, Dee, DJ, my sister and nephew, and I made plans to meet outside his apartment on a random afternoon. No turning back now, faking sick, or using Chicago traffic as an excuse to reschedule. For someone who'd always encouraged others to face their challenges head-on and in a direct fashion, had you looked up the definition of hypocrite online, you would've found a picture of me highlighted as an example on that day. I never told her, but having my sister there meant everything. For her, it was probably just another visit since she'd had a long and positive relationship with my father, but for me, she was the lifeline that kept me from drowning as I inched closer to his entryway. Love you, Quita.

My arms had never felt heavier than they did as I reached for the doorbell. It'd been nearly a decade and a half since I'd seen or spoken to him, and not knowing what to expect on the other side of the door, the only emotion I could identify was sheer and absolute terror. The last time I saw my father, he seemed ten feet tall, weighed a thousand pounds, and had a voice that could shake a building. But then the door creaked open, and there he stood: the same man I had feared and resented for so long, but... different. I had three inches and twenty pounds on him. For the first time, I saw him not as a monster, but as a man with flaws.

After we stumbled into a handshake that awkwardly turned into a hug, I walked through the door and began the long, labor intensive work of letting bygones be bygones. He met DJ for the first time, whispered a quiet hello to Jordyn, who was still growing inside Dee's belly, and then spent three hours catching up on everything and nothing. As much as I'd like to say my disdain for the man ruined any chance of reconciliation, I can't. Truth is, I enjoyed that time. It brought me a peace I didn't know I needed and made me believe I had what it took to be a good father or, at least, gave me a better idea of where to start. Looking back, I just wish I hadn't waited so long to reach out.

Mom's Moment

Two months before I reunited with my dad, my eldest niece was getting ready to graduate from high school in a small town in southern Illinois. My relationship with her mom—my oldest sister (not to be confused with the one who supported me through my visit with our father)—was strained and distant. Even with that tension, nothing was going to stop me from showing up to celebrate my niece's accomplishments. I may have only been ten when she was born, but in my eyes, she was my first child and I promised myself I would do or be whatever she needed because she deserved all the good this world could offer.

I booked our hotel rooms, rented a giant passenger van, and packed it with love and noise. Uncle Mike rode up front with me. Dee, DJ, and a few bags filled the next row. My baby sisters were behind them with my niece Alana, who was only two at the time. And bringing up the rear were my mom and Mr. Strader, her partner and our unofficial but very official stepfather. The trip there, graduation, and family dinner that followed all went off without a hitch. For two and a half days, it felt like we had managed to show up for each other, laughing, telling stories, and genuinely enjoying being in each other's company. For a moment, I let myself believe we'd pull off this whole trip without a single emotional bruise. But the elders have a saying about what happens to people who assume...

On the morning we were set to pack up and head home, my mom and oldest sister got into a massive fight. And I don't mean the loud, passive aggressive kind of disagreement most families have. I mean the kind where, if I didn't grab one of them and physically remove her from the room, I'd be compelled to testify at the subsequent murder trial. After the dust settled, we loaded into the van and started the drive back to Minnesota, but the energy that had once joyfully lifted us a mere twenty-four hours ago had completely disappeared. In its place? Silence, tension, and unmovable emotional baggage. Though we'd spent the ride down to Illinois singing old school R&B, I was perfectly content to drive in that awkward quiet for the next seven hours back home. My mother, however, had different plans.

My younger sisters and I already knew how this went. When our mother felt something, she wanted everyone around her to feel it too. If she was happy, you were expected to be happy. If she was sad, then we all had to be sad with her. And if you didn't match her emotional state, she would do whatever it took to correct the imbalance. True to form, she made sure everyone in that van was just as miserable as she was, picking fights with anyone who looked her way, unnecessarily lingering at rest stops to prolong the agony of the car ride, and pushing buttons she knew would set people off. Anything to tip the emotional scales in her direction. Our collective blood pressure rose to dangerous levels, and I'm still not sure how we made it home without that van turning into a crime scene.

By some miracle, we reached the final stretch, and the tension had cooled just enough for me to exhale. As I glanced up at the rearview mirror trying to see what was going on in the backseat, I caught a glimpse of my mom blankly staring out the window. Something was off, but my only focus was on completing the final half hour of the hellish voyage. When we finally pulled up to her apartment, I braked hard and threw the van into park with a little extra force. My not-so-subtle way of saying, "You can get out now," but she didn't move. She couldn't. My sisters started to panic, but I just assumed (there's that word again...) she'd taken drugs at one of the stops and was now high as a kite. I figured she was in a fog and would snap out of it soon enough.

But one ambulance ride, three surgeries, a ventriculostomy, feeding tube, and a weeklong medically induced coma later, we learned the truth. My mother had suffered a massive stroke. A vein in her brain had ruptured, likely triggered by the spikes in blood pressure from the fight that morning and elevated heart rate throughout the trip home. She now requires round the clock monitoring and "lives" in a care facility as a shell of her former self. Right arm: completely limp. Right leg: only partially functional. Unable to effectively communicate and possessing the cognitive reasoning skills of a ten-year-old.

Since that fateful trip, my relationship with my mother has been complicated in every way. Sometimes she presents as a vulnerable adult in need of compassion and patience, and on those days, I feel deep sorrow that her final years are being lived out in a nursing home as the world keeps moving without her. And sometimes, I feel anger (or at least a nagging sense of manipulation) as she shows glimmers of the woman she used to be. Like the time she stole Mr. Strader's car keys and went joyriding, paying no mind to her inability to move the right side of her body or the countless other reasons she shouldn't have been behind the wheel.

Still, I visit her every Sunday, bringing her a big plate of barbecue, a case of her favorite drink, and spending a little time catching up on what's new. When I'm in need of affirmation, I linger in the hallway just long enough to receive the inevitable remarks one of the several nurses toss my way, "Your mom is so lucky to have you and your sisters." They tell me I must be "the best guy in the world," that my love and consistency are unmatched, sharing stories about how other residents are jealous of all the food, photos, and gifts we bring on a regular basis. They smile when I walk in because they expect I'm delivering joy with a side of ribs. But they have no idea; completely unaware that with every visit, I'm trying to convince myself that the argument in that van didn't contribute to the stroke. That my words, my anger, my inability to disengage didn't play a role in what happened to her brain. I'm still not sure. I may never be.

Tragedy number one.

Alone

Despite my best intentions but undeniably less-than-best efforts, my dad and I fell out of touch again. We exchanged a few messages on social media and sent a couple texts, but that faded after a few months. Was I disappointed? Maybe. I don't know. Reconnecting had felt meaningful at the time, but I'd also learned how to live without him, and if I'm honest, this time around I was probably more responsible for the distance than he was.

About a year and a half later, I was home alone. Dee was out getting a pedicure, and the kids were at her parents' house for the afternoon. I had a rare window of freedom and did what any millennial dad would: picked up the game controller and jumped headfirst into a post-apocalyptic world, slaying zombies and scavenging for enough supplies to prepare for the boss fight. I was mid-level, fully immersed, gearing up for the final showdown when my phone rang.

Immediately, I thought, *Uh oh. This must be bad. Who even calls anymore? Haven't they heard of texting?* I looked down and saw Grandpa TC's name glowing on the screen. *Phew*, I thought, *It's just Grandpa. One of the few people left who still refuses to text. All good. False alarm.* I answered the phone with my usual affectionate excitement, but I could hear something was off in his voice. "Son, I don't know how to tell you this, so I'm just gonna say it. Your dad passed away. Heart attack. They found him in his apartment a few days later."

The first five or six years of my life, I was glued to my dad's side. And no matter how much trauma came with exposure to drugs, guns, violence, and the occasional tiptoeing across eggshells or navigating through emotional minefields, I was still a little boy who just wanted his father. From ages seven to twelve, he was in and out of my life, as he bounced between apartments and prison. But from twelve to twenty-eight, I settled into the reality that I'd never have the movie version of a father-son bond. Just wounds and what ifs. Still, when Grandpa TC gave me the news, all I could do was collapse into a corner and weep, sobbing like the little boy I used to be who just wanted to protect his parent. Only this time, it was for my father.

Dee and I planned a weeklong trip to Chicago so I could say goodbye, and on the drive down, my mind spun in circles, obsessing over what would be expected of me. As his only son, I knew people would look to me to speak at the service and that thought sat heavy on my chest as I wondered what I would say about a man I hadn't truly known during the most formative years of my life. *What stories should I share? What truth could I tell that wouldn't dishonor him or betray myself?* I played with the idea of doing what people do in movies: start reading the safe, polished remarks I'd prepared, then stop, crumble the paper dramatically, and spitefully speak from the heart. But that idea disappeared the moment I saw Grandma Nancy.

No parent ever expects to bury their child. That's not how the story's supposed to go. We bring children into the world hoping to raise them strong enough to survive long after we're gone, and for Grandma Nancy, it didn't matter that my dad had made it into his fifties or that he'd hurt people in his life along the way. In that moment, the only relevant detail was that she had to bury her baby, and the weight of that grief is something no parent should ever carry.

I walked into the church wearing a black suit, shirt, sunglasses, and blue striped tie, a nod to one of his favorite colors, suggested by Quita. As I made my way to the casket, I noticed people doing doubletakes when they caught a glimpse of me. "Damn, you look just like your daddy. Thought you were him for a second." I heard it again and again, and each time, felt a strange mix of shame and pride. I replied with, "thank you," because... I didn't know what else to say.

When it was my turn to pay respects, I went alone. The kids weren't ready for the sight of a dead body, and if there was one thing I learned from my father's missteps, it was to be mindful of what I exposed my children to. I leaned over the casket and felt... nothing. Not because I didn't care or harbored anger, but because the man lying there didn't look like my dad. After being found days later, and with the amount of reconstruction that had to be done, his face looked like a stranger's. It was surreal. Maybe I should have felt something else but seeing him in that way oddly gave me strength. I told myself I needed to be the rock and hold others up. So that's what I did. Literally. For forty-five minutes, I walked cousins, aunts, and friends up to the casket, embraced them in my arms to keep them upright as they crumbled to the floor, whispered loving words of encouragement, helped them to their seats, and turned around and did it all over again. And again. And again.

Then it was time to approach the podium and grab ahold of the microphone that'd been taunting me from the moment I stepped foot inside the church. I was the last person to speak before the pastor gave his final word, which created a metaphoric pressure so intense that it transformed the lump of coal in my throat into diamond-quality remarks, mixing the complex nature of our challenging relationship while acknowledging the hardship of losing a loved one. I talked about how imperfect we all are, yet how we're also exactly who we are meant to be. I thanked my father for teaching me to be a fighter (figuratively and literally), touched on doing the best we can with the hands we're dealt, joked about his love for strawberry milk and trivia gameshows, and somehow, in all of that, found the closure I needed. But later, I couldn't shake one thought: my father died alone in his apartment. I couldn't help but draw a straight line between that and the fear I carried; the fear that if I ever messed up too badly, if I ever hurt Dee or the kids beyond repair, that I'd end up the same way. Alone, reluctantly mourned, and unrecognizable.

Tragedy number two.

Measured Response

My mother met Mr. Strader in 2003, not long after moving to Minnesota from Chicago. He was sharp, confident, and put together; a man with financial stability and just enough charm to fill every corner of a room. He had been a carpenter for decades and was now teaching the craft to the next generation. There was never a project he couldn't tackle, but what stood out most was how he poured that same energy into people. He saw something in my mother that few others could. While the world might have looked at her and seen a homeless single mom battling addiction, Mr. Strader looked deeper and saw a survivor. A fighter. A woman who had been to hell and back and was somehow still standing. That, I think, is what he admired most. Her fight. Lord knows she fought and unfortunately, it was usually him on the receiving end of it.

For fifteen years, he uplifted our family, looking out for my sisters and me like we were his own and giving his time, energy, love, and money. And for fifteen years, my mother drained him, stealing from his wallet, selling his tools, wiping out his accounts, and manipulating him in every way possible to get what she wanted, no matter the cost. And yet, he stayed. Even after the stroke, he never left her side, continuing to pour into a cup that would never be full. As a carpenter, he taught me that sometimes the best course of action was to roll up my sleeves and prepare for the hard but necessary work it took to fix a problem, teaching me to measure ten times and cut once. My mother, unfortunately, was a well-worn room for which he was ill equipped to renovate.

On a random weekday in February 2019, I got a call from the hospital saying Mr. Strader had been admitted to the intensive care unit, reporting that his symptoms were serious and possibly life threatening. The next day, however, Dee called his hospital room to get an update from the nurses and could hear him in the background, laughing and talking to anyone who would listen. Apparently, he was demanding more food and complaining about the temperature in the room. Classic Mr. Strader. His energy was strong, voice was full, and it sounded like he'd be back on his feet in no time.

I made plans to visit the next day to celebrate his recovery but when I walked into the room, a doctor met me at the door with a look on her face that told me everything I didn't want to hear. "His organs are shutting down and he only has a few hours left," she said. "How?" I uncharacteristically yelled before elaborating further in my head, *He was just walking around and demanding more criminally under-seasoned Salisbury steak the other day and now you're saying he's going to die?*

She nodded gently and sat me down. "Are you familiar with terminal lucidity?" she asked. I wasn't. "It's commonly known as 'the surge,'" she explained, "It's a period of increased energy and alertness that some patients experience hours or days before they pass away. It's almost like the body's attempt at one last jump start before letting go." I immediately called my sisters and Dee and told them to come as quickly as possible. But just when we thought things were already as bad as they could be, we were hit with an impossible ultimatum.

"If his heart stops again," the doctor said, "we can try CPR, but in his condition, it's likely to break ribs and cause significant suffering. Or…" We waited as if the second half of her sentence would present a better, more comforting option. "…we can take him off life support now and let him pass peacefully." We froze. I felt everyone's eyes shift toward me as they gave me the responsibility of saying the words they couldn't bring themselves to.

"Teron… what are we going to do?" I was petrified. I wasn't old or wise enough for this. In the movies, people making these decisions are supposed to be in their fifties and I was about twenty-five years too early. Stalling, I asked, "Are you sure his body can't fight back? Are you sure the machines are the only thing keeping him here? Are there really no other options?" The doctor nodded again.

Fearing the additional pain we might selfishly cause for a few extra moments and hating ourselves for having to choose, our hearts broke as we gave consent to remove our most consistent father figure from life support. Gathered around his bed, we thanked him for loving us like his own, held his hand, whispered our goodbyes, and gave him permission to rest as his chest deflated for the last time. The room filled with grief and wails of despair as we collapsed around him, overcome with sorrow, wondering if we had made the right call. I don't know about anyone else, but I'm still debating it. Love you, Mr. Strader.

Number three. Halfway there…

Imperfect Timing

Almost exactly one year later, we got hit with one of the biggest snowstorms in recent memory. Most people would consider that a nightmare, but I couldn't have been happier. Snow, to me, is more than just frozen inconvenience. It's a symbol of the season and a time for care, giving, and gratitude. I actually get a little sad when we don't get enough of it and dread the idea of a gray Christmas. I. Love. Snow. Back at our first house, our next-door neighbor had this top tier, two stage snow blower that could clear an entire block like it was nothing. He'd go up and down the street, removing a little bit of burden from every house along the way. I always thanked him for his kindness and vowed to myself that one day, I'd be "that guy" if the opportunity ever presented itself. And it didn't take long. I purchased a beastly machine similar to his, and in our current neighborhood, I'm known as the guy who wakes up early and clears a path for schoolkids, joggers, dog walkers, and mail carriers alike. But if I'm being real, I do it mostly for me. It gives me a sense of purpose and pride. A kind of quiet joy.

So, when the big storm hit, I was ready. I had the gear, a plan, and motivation. I'd been waiting and training for this moment. In my mind, this was the championship game with seconds left on the clock, down one with the ball in my hands. El Toro Loco (my imaginary snow removal coach) was in my head yelling that this was what we had worked for and that our time had finally come. Before I could take the final shot, however, Dee called me inside. I could hear something different in her voice, something serious, so I dropped everything and came running. She didn't bury the lede. "Your sister just called. Grandma Nancy isn't doing too well. You need to go see her. It's 11:30 a.m. The next flight leaves at 1:00 p.m. After that, the only other one is at 3:30 p.m." That's one of the many things I love about Dee; she doesn't waste time. She handles what needs handling. Always has.

I was nervous about the roads. The snow was coming down hard, and I didn't want to risk missing the earlier flight, so I booked the 3:30 p.m. departure, packed my bag, collected my thoughts, and headed to the airport. The only available seat was in first class, which made my poor kid instincts flinch but not falter. Ticket in hand and anxiety cranked up to eleven, I impatiently waited as the screens above the gate updated. "Delayed. Delayed. Cancelled. Delayed." The storm had shut everything down. My flight was now pushed to 6:45 p.m., and even that wasn't guaranteed. Worried I might miss the window to speak with my grandmother one last time, I called Grandpa TC and asked him to put me on speaker. I'd been texting with Quita all afternoon. I knew Grandma Nancy couldn't talk, but she could still listen.

"Hey, lady. It's Teron. I'm on my way. I'm just a little delayed, but I'll be there soon." I didn't tell her about the storm. No need to give her something else to worry about. "Oh, and don't worry about coaching tonight. I've got it covered." That was our thing. She was the imaginary head coach of our hometown basketball team, and during our weekly calls, we'd plan out game strategies, talk lineups, and decide how to rally the team when they inevitably fell behind by twenty points. Total nonsense, but it was *our* nonsense. "If it's alright with you," I said, "I'm going to make a couple changes to the rotation. Let some of the guys on the bench get some minutes to see what we've got for next season." Grandpa TC got back on the phone to tell me that she, through a small smile and head nod, had given her approval. "And I know this might be weird for one coach to say to another" I finished, "but... I love you. With everything I've got and then some. I'll see you soon."

The flight, now set for 6:45 p.m., finally boarded. The trip was short—only forty-five minutes—but felt like an eternity. I turned on airplane mode and sat in the dark quiet of the cabin, disconnected from everything and everyone I cared about, and as the snow-covered ground vanished beneath us, I felt the ache in my chest grow heavier with each passing mile. When we landed, I stared at and tapped on my phone as I waited for it to catch up on all the updates that'd undoubtedly been sent while I was unreachable. With no missed calls or unread messages, I clung tightly to the adage that *no* news was *good* news as a wave of relief started to build. That is, until the other shoe dropped in the form of a text message from Dee that simply read, "I'm so sorry."

I didn't need clarification. I knew. Grandma Nancy passed away while I was in the air. When I arrived, she was still lying in her bed. Quita requested for her to be kept in place until I got there, giving me a chance to say a proper goodbye. Understanding the depth of our connection, Grandpa TC asked everyone to leave the room so that I could have a private moment with her. I tried to quiet my cries as I kneeled beside her, bargaining with the universe for a shot at a do over. I didn't want much;

just another second to thank the woman who had made sure we never went without a merry Christmas or Thanksgiving meal. To admire the fighter who had already beaten cancer once and was one of the strongest, fiercest, most loving people I had ever known. If anyone could come back, it would be her. Right? Please?

A week later, there I was again: standing at another podium, giving another speech. I told the congregation to hold tight to the recollections. That every joke, every meal, every hard truth she ever delivered was now a part of us. I reminded them that the best way to keep her alive was to live out those memories. I shared a story from college when, during my freshman year, I told Grandma about Dee and how I thought I'd found "the one." She was thrilled, and after the usual words of grandmotherly encouragement, hit me with a curveball. "Are you practicing responsible and safe intimacy?" I froze. "No, Grandma," I stammered. "I mean, yes. I mean, we're not doing anything like that. We're waiting until marriage. No need to worry- there won't be any mini me's running around."

Four years later when Dee and I called to let her know we'd gotten engaged, she was finally presented with the opportunity to let loose an exclamation I can only assume she'd been sitting on for nearly half of a decade: "oh, so you're ready for some sex now!?" I tended to have a comeback on deck for awkward instances like these but was completely shaken in that moment. I could only embarrassingly screech back "grandma!" as we heartily laughed long enough to induce unrelenting headaches. Totally worth it.

A few weeks after the funeral, the world shut down. COVID

was everywhere, and I had more idle time on my hands than I'd had in years. My anxious mind didn't know what to do with itself, so I started rewatching my life like an old film, scene by scene, moment by moment. Some thoughts were small and ridiculous, *Remember that conversation you had with that one random stranger on the bus a decade ago when you mistakenly said, "could care less" instead of "couldn't care less?" You think that guy noticed? Think he's still judging you all these years later?* Probably not, but maybe. At other times, the thoughts hit harder. *If you had booked the 1:00 p.m. flight... you would have been in the air by three... and maybe you would've made it in time to be with her in those final moments....*

Can I stop counting now?

Thankful?

After my mom decided it was time for me to move to Minnesota, Uncle Mike returned to the south side of Chicago for a while before moving in with my cousin, Ebony. Over the next decade and a half, their bond evolved into what it had always been destined to become: less uncle and niece, more father and daughter. They had been through storms and sunshine, wins and losses, tears and laughter. And every time they came out stronger, closer, and with a dozen new inside jokes to carry them through the next wave.

About a year and a half after Grandma Nancy passed, Uncle Mike came down with a nasty case of shingles, spotlighted by painful rashes and swollen welts across his torso. Ebony and I spent hours on the phone trying to convince him to go to the hospital, but he was stubborn, asserting he'd had shingles before and could tough it out again. By January 2022, the pain had gotten so bad he finally agreed to let Ebony take him to the emergency room. They treated the rash but noticed the welts didn't quite line up with a typical shingles diagnosis. They ran tests, drew blood and took tissue samples, attempting to make sense of what his body was trying to tell them. A week later, we got results no one was prepared to receive- stage four gallbladder cancer. The welts were tumors that had metastasized throughout his body, and while there were treatments that might minutely extend his life, the outlook was grim. Another flight and a few hours later, I was on the ground and ready to support, console, game plan, and help however I could.

I don't want to speculate about the hospital's staff, but I'll say this- it felt like he wasn't getting the care he needed in Chicago. The doctors had him on an oral chemotherapy drug that made him violently ill, inducing nausea almost immediately after taking it. Now, I'm no expert, but I've watched enough medical dramas to know that if the medication always ends up in the toilet, the chances of it doing its job are pretty low. He was wasting away. In less than a year, he lost almost half his body weight, his appetite had vanished, and the small bits he managed to choke down rarely stayed. Ebony and I had several conversations and eventually agreed to have him stay with Dee and me in Minnesota for a bit while we sought additional care options. A change of scenery. A second opinion. A new shot at hope.

And at first, it seemed to work. I don't know if it was the fresh start, quality of care, or our desire to believe things were getting better, but within weeks we had him set up with a new primary doctor, an infectious disease specialist, IV chemo, physical therapy, occupational therapy...everything. We leaned into expectancy hard, and even though we knew better, we let ourselves believe we could buy more time. But the chemo had side effects. Violent ones. His diaphragm would spasm, and when it did, he couldn't breathe. For twenty or thirty seconds at a time, he'd flail and kick, trying to force air into lungs that refused to cooperate. Every time it happened, I held my breath and thought, *This is it. This is the one that takes him.*

The only option that helped came in the form of a strong muscle relaxer but was also accompanied by its own set of issues, often causing him to sleep all day and wake up lethargic and completely zapped. So, while we avoided the breathless panic attacks, we traded it for constant fatigue, an absent desire to eat, and insufficient energy for therapies.

And here's where it gets hard to write because, while I love(d) Uncle Mike, things got complicated once he joined our household. I thought that taking him in meant I would be his caregiver and he would trust me completely. That he would follow my lead and let me make the hard choices. And maybe he did. But I was too rigid. Too intense. I wanted him to eat full meals, sleep at regular hours, exercise every day, and take every dose of every prescription. I was so focused on what I thought was best that I never stopped to ask how my "care" felt to him. I didn't see how heavy I had become. I thought I was helping, but in reality, I was forcing him to outrun death on a treadmill while he could no longer walk. If I believed he wasn't getting *enough* from his doctors in Chicago, then maybe it followed that he was getting *too much* from me.

Things fell apart in October 2022. His appetite was gone, and he refused most meals, opting instead for cookies, snack cakes, ice cream sandwiches, mints, crackers, candy, anything but real food. I was furious. *How am I supposed to help him heal if he doesn't follow the plan? Can't he see I'm trying to save him? How do I care more about his life than he does?* I now realize how unfair that line of questioning was, but at that moment, I couldn't see it. We had a huge argument that ended with him saying he wanted to go back to Chicago. He had threatened that before, but this time, I knew he meant it and I didn't have the fortitude to fight.

Dee and I packed his things, labeled his meds, loaded the car, and drove him the six hours to Ebony's, only stopping for gas. When we arrived, she could tell something had shifted between us, and having lived with him for so long, understood how much of a handful he could be. I took solace in knowing I wasn't the only one who could become so irritated with him that my lid nearly popped, but I was still saddened beyond belief. Before leaving, I begrudgingly marched up to and stared at Uncle Mike until his only option was to meet my gaze, gave him a hug and told him I loved him. As I walked out the door and down the steps, I wiped away tears and settled on the understanding that that'd be the last time I saw him alive.

But I was wrong. Sort of. He called a week later and we laid it all out on the table. I apologized for being too militant and he thanked me for doing my best in a situation that had no easy answers. Three weeks later, Ebony called, barely holding herself together. Through tears she'd informed me he had checked himself into hospice, and with that one line, completely shattered my world. Another packed bag, purchased ticket, and somber flight. At this rate, it probably makes more sense to lease a jet, right?

When I got to the hospice center, he was barely conscious. The medications had him so sedated he couldn't speak or move without immense effort. With few meaningful options left, I figured the only role I could play was that of a message courier. I stayed with him as long as the facility permitted, talked with nurses, and video called family who couldn't travel to be there in person. Like with Grandma Nancy, I quietly asked him to reconsider his decision, even though we both knew there was no other reasonable choice left.

After a few days, I made the call to return home. I was able to catch a flight the Wednesday night before Thanksgiving, because if I knew anything about Uncle Mike, it was that he would have wanted me to be with Dee and the kids on the one day we were supposed to intentionally set aside to practice gratitude. I got off the plane and immediately collapsed into bed. The emotional toll had turned physical, forcing my body to shut down and culminating with a ten hour "nap." I was finally getting the rest I needed, but as the theme of this entire section has illustrated, what goes up must come down. Most people wake up to an alarm, child, sunlight, or an internal compulsion to get out of bed. Not me. The following morning, I woke up to a missed call from Ebony, which resulted in me spending the bulk of Thanksgiving evening writing yet another eulogy. Why couldn't I just let him eat the damn ice cream sandwich?

After Uncle Mike, I lulled myself into believing I was in the clear. I'd lived through my fair share of loss and could finally stop peeking around the corner waiting for the next tragedy to strike. If you'd asked me, I was all paid up, mathematically convinced that I'd ended my go-rounds with saying farewell to loved ones and anyone who might try to convince me otherwise could expect swift and violent consequences and repercussions. The arithmetic— death usually comes in threes. Ok, cool. My dad, Mr. Strader, Grandma Nancy, and Uncle Mike. That's four! And although she was still alive, my mother's condition had catastrophically compromised her quality of life, which had to count for at least half a point, right? Based on that logic, I was actually *owed* a bit of good fortune. Couple that with the fact that no one else in my circle was sick, old, weak, or any of the other descriptors that usually precede death, and it all made sense to me. Mathematically, ya know? But when you forget to carry the one, factor in confounding variables, or remember that fate sometimes has a cruel way of changing the formula, you might end up with an anomaly on your hands.

One more to go…

Standing Room Only

I was at a conference in Indiana in late October 2023. Nothing flashy or special. I'd attended every year, meeting up with friends and colleagues to level-set on how we might deliver products and services more cohesively and consistently for our valued customers. The event ran from Friday morning through Saturday afternoon, but coming from Minnesota, I had to catch a flight Thursday evening to ensure I'd arrive on time and be ready for the busy weekend ahead.

DJ and Jordyn, knowing this trip marked the beginning of my hectic travel season, made it particularly hard to leave. I'd somehow managed to convince them I was an exceptional and extraordinary father, worthy of their admiration, respect, and emotional capital, but their unwillingness to let me go was part of the cost that came with that crown. Their protest and worry about me leaving were amplified by a field trip they'd be taking at day camp while school was closed for a two-day fall break. The outing would require them to step outside their comfort zones and show up in a space that didn't exactly scream "safety."

I did my best to reassure them everything would be just fine. I encouraged them to go in with good attitudes and curiously bold mindsets, playing up the benefits of participating and re-minding them that life would be filled with new experiences and opportunities that could broaden their perspectives and help build their character. Oh, and did I forget to mention the field trip was to a scaled down amusement park? Yeah... Based on their buildup, you'd think they were headed into some kind of treacherous unknown. More accurately, it was just an unfamiliar park with a few climbing areas, spiraling slides, and more swings than you could count. But somehow it had just enough mystery to stir up worry about what should've been a fun and exciting time. Unrelated— I hear scientists are finding more and more evidence that anxiety might actually be passed down from par-ents to their children. Can't blame Dee for this one....

Try as I did, I couldn't get them to let their guards down. Thankfully I wasn't fighting that battle alone. In addition to Dee's nurturing spirit and consistently positive outlook, we had

Papa. That was the name DJ and Jordyn gave Dee's dad once they were old enough to form the words. He'd refused to go by "Grandpa" because it made him feel older than he believed himself to be. "Big Papa" got shut down quickly by Dee, Meemo (Dee's mom), and me because there was no way we were giving that kind of ego boost room to grow. We landed on "Papa," simple and agreeable to everyone.

Dee talked to her dad every single morning at 8:30 a.m. sharp. Without fail, her phone would ring at that exact time, and I never had to wonder who was on the other end. If I didn't have a watch or phone nearby, I could use their ritual as a way to tell time. Like clockwork, the unique ringtone for video calls would chime, and their conversation would follow the same familiar rhythm. Dee answered with an enthusiastic "sup?" He'd comment on how wild her hair looked. She'd tell him to shut up. They'd laugh, reflect on yesterday, and walk each other through the plans for the day ahead.

The morning of my trip was a little different. Since the kids had the day off from school, Dee had to walk them into the day camp, which was inside a well-known fitness center. To her surprise and delight, Papa was there working out. That had kind of become his thing. Ever since retiring from his long career, he'd taken a more active approach to life. Lifting weights, doing cardio, paying closer attention to what he ate. Investing in himself and committing to sticking around for the long haul.

The kids spotted him on a stationary bike and took off sprinting like they'd just won the lottery. I mean, they moved with crackhead level speed (relax; I can say it) and tackled him with hugs that probably felt like full on chokeholds. He asked how they were doing, and without pause, they spilled every ounce of their fieldtrip concerns. By the time they wrapped up their chat, you wouldn't have guessed they'd been worried at all, even having come up with a little song to sing about their newfound excitement and carefree spirit. That was Papa. He had a way of making people feel better. Didn't matter if it was a stranger at the grocery store, a friend at dinner, a grandkid having a hard day, or simply showing off his uncanny ability to make Dee genuinely laugh by simply instructing her to do so. He made people's days better by being in them.

Part one of the conference went as expected. Learned a few things, talked to some people, networked a bit, ate a little dinner, and headed to my room to recover from all the social interaction before falling asleep. Around 2:00 a.m., my phone rang. It was Dee. Knowing that she's rarely up that late and under the belief she'd never interrupt my fleeting sleep unless it was urgent, I knew something had to be wrong. Dee confirmed my suspicion by letting me know Papa had suffered a heart attack and was rushed to the hospital. As had become tradition for me the past few years, I scrambled to find a flight.

Over the next week, Papa was heavily sedated and connected to several machines that worked overtime to help his body rebound from the cardiac event. Dee and James spent every visiting hour at his side, comforting Meemo and sending me updates throughout the day. On a couple occasions she offered to switch places with me so I could visit while she stayed with the kids, but I declined. I exaggerated my wish for her to be with him and insisted Papa would not want me to see him that way, because I couldn't admit the truth: I didn't have the strength to watch one of the strongest men I knew lie so vulnerable. I had already watched too many loved ones wait for death to decide whether it'd show mercy or claim another pillar of my life. I couldn't face it again.

After Covid, we enrolled DJ and Jordyn in a math and reading program because we didn't want them falling behind in their coursework. Twice a week they attended sessions in person. Normally Dee and I shared driving duties, but that week I took both shifts. DJ finished early, so I let him play on his tablet in the back seat while I waited in the parking lot for Jordyn. When Dee called, I assumed it was the usual update. I was wrong.

"He's gone," she sobbed. "The doctors said he's gone." I'm usually levelheaded, but not then. The words hit, and I snapped, "You're a [expletive] liar," before hanging up. It felt as though a stranger had told me *my* father had died, and I lashed out at the messenger— my wife, Papa's daughter. Realizing my mistake, I stepped out of the car and called back to apologize, comfort Dee, and grasp what had happened. Honestly, I was less interested in details and more concerned with confirming I hadn't misheard. Denial let me cling to a thread of faith. *By "gone," did she mean he had rallied, been discharged, and was on his way home?* She didn't.

Say what you want about screentime addiction in children, but on the fifteen-minute car ride from the learning center to our house, I needed them to be full-on junkies. I'd tried to repurpose my deep despair and sorrow into physical strength by gripping the steering wheel as tightly as possible but couldn't account for my heart's desire to simply weep. With headphones plugged in and full attention directed at their tablets, the kids hadn't a clue in the world what'd just happened. I'd aimed to keep it that way until Dee got home and we were ready to break the news together. That's a funny word, *Ready*. They'd never experienced the loss of an immediate family member, and though I'd had training in helping other folks' kids deal with grief and trauma, we didn't really have a framework to reference as we laid out the full truth for ours. We damn near dehydrated from all the crying that ensued.

During the days that followed, our homes filled with loved ones from every corner of the country. Some stayed a few days, others much longer, and together we grieved the sudden loss of a man who shaped us all. Food lost its taste, sleep came in fits, and moods swung from hollow sorrow to molten rage. Want to know what helps with grief? Walking through it with people you love. Want to know what doesn't help? Punching your home office door so hard that you leave a baseball sized hole for everyone to see. But what's a few bruised knuckles and trips to the hardware store when you've tried your best to be "on" for everyone else and forgotten to give yourself the appropriate space to authentically feel your feelings?

On the morning of the funeral, I put on the darkest sunglasses I owned, knowing my eyes were so red they would alarm anyone who looked too closely. I volunteered to drive, thinking a task might distract me, but instead it gave my tears a larger audience. Meemo sat behind me and watched the steady stream run down my face in the mirror. She reached out her hand to rub my shoulder as if to say, *it's ok; we're going to be ok.* That was it. The straw that broke the camel's back. Every bit of resolve I had built up inside immediately slipped away. She'd just lost her husband, partner, and best friend of nearly four decades and *she* was consoling *me*? It was too much to bear. Too much to process. Too much to hold back. At a red light, I put my head on the steering wheel in a signal of defeat. I'd lost the battle of trying to be the calm within the storm, and Meemo knew it. She didn't have to utter a word; a simple hand on the shoulder said everything.

I sat at the front of the church with the rest of the immediate family: DJ, Jordyn, Meemo, James, Lauren (James' wife), Everett and Rowan (my nephews), and Dee. From that spot I saw how each one needed something slightly different to get through the service. Appointing myself the emotional sponge, I tried to meet those needs before they spilled over: a clutch of tissues, a quick nod, a firm hand squeeze, a shoulder ready for tears. Whatever the moment called for, I offered it. Before the service, Meemo asked me to speak on behalf of the family. I hesitated, doubting I was the right vessel, but her unwavering trust settled it. Focused on those beside me, I hadn't noticed that more than four hundred fifty people had filled every seat, with more still trickling in. Fire marshal be damned; we were fitting everyone.

The pastor kindly asked each speaker to keep their remarks to under two minutes, and for most, that was a fair request, but I was not most. As the closer, I felt obliged to bring the house down. For sixteen minutes I painted a picture of the man we loved, how far he had come, and how his relationships looked from my vantage point. He started off as "Mr. Prioleau," a protective father who, upon meeting me for the first time, skipped over the greeting and immediately challenged me to a urine test in the basement. He later became "Dee's dad," a father who, regardless of how old she got, would always refer to his daughter as "baby girl" and be at her side in a moment's notice. Then, "my father-in-law," trusting and welcoming me into his family's inner circle when all the conventional wisdom and movies warned otherwise. Afterward, a soon-to-be grandfather who literally attempted to track down the anesthesiologist and drag him back to the room where Dee had been waiting for an epidural. And finally, "Papa," the ever present and loving grandfather every child deserves to have but few actually get.

But, more than anything, he was... him. Steven. Sure, he talked a good game and tried to put on a tough guy mask every now and again, but he was a total teddy bear inside. Like any parent, he possessed the ability to flip a switch and go into supreme protector mode if needed, but more times than not, he ended up being the guy who gave sage advice and guidance while leaving just enough space for us to learn on our own and secretly providing a safety net just in case. The guy who had spent nearly thirty years coaching youth girls' basketball, providing them with more than just an athletic outlet or legacy of winning, but also the skills needed to succeed in the part of life that takes place off the court. It's funny, to pass time I sometimes think about what a person's superpower might be if their greatest characteristic was given an astronomical boost. You might think Papa's would be super strength, some sort of healing ability, or telepathy. Not me. Given a choice, I'd pick teleportation. Why? It's simple— he was always exactly where we needed him *when* we needed him. Even from the afterlife, he seems to show up at just the right moments with subtle reminders that he's still watching over, smiling down on, and looking out for us.

LESSONS LEARNED PART 5

B Y THE TIME I was twenty-seven years old, I'd only ever been to one funeral. Granny's. And that was when I was twelve. All things considered, I should probably see myself as one of the "lucky ones." A lot of folks who come from backgrounds like mine find themselves trapped in the revolving doors of funeral homes, hospital bedsides, and church pews, saying goodbye to loved ones, many far earlier than anyone should ever have to. And while I understand that my sorrow doesn't need to be comparable to anyone else's in order to be valid, I'd be remiss if I didn't acknowledge that fifteen-year window of relative serenity.

Ages twenty-seven through thirty-five told a completely different story. Over those never-ending years, I witnessed a life shattering accident that took away my mother's independence, authored and curated three heart wrenching obituaries, and delivered what I believe to be the funeral equivalent of a keynote speech five times in eight years. Any luck I'd had up until that point had clearly been depleted, feeling like I'd have to rely solely on preparation, ambition, skill, and hard work to get through the next chapters of life. Gross. Who does that? One out of ten. Would not recommend.

But by now you know me pretty well, so it probably won't surprise you to learn that I eventually found a way to sport those ridiculously optimistic and exuberantly rose-colored glasses once more. In classic Teron fashion, I forced myself to look for the silver lining that exists somewhere between crippling tragedy and glorious triumph. And while it might not always be enough to completely lift me from the slump that comes with remembering any deep loss, it's comforting to believe that a lesson might be found if we know where to look.

Transference Of Energy

My mother was steeped in instability. Granny did all she could to provide a positive home environment, but my mother's formative years were spent experimenting with drugs and living a fast and loose lifestyle. I don't blame her, though. I can't. She was battling demons that most of us will never have to acknowledge even exist and needed a way to numb the unrelenting pain heaped onto her at nearly every turn. When she met my father, that instability shifted into something more like a Stockholm syndrome dependency. She gained a bit more consistency and stability, but at the cost of her mental, physical, and emotional health. Their relationship was mutually parasitic in more ways than I can count, and even after she broke free, she never embraced relationships in a way that didn't involve calculating how she might "get over" on whoever dared to love her out loud.

After her stroke and catastrophic regression, my sisters and I couldn't help but wonder if things would have been different had we not gone on that trip to my niece's graduation or chose an alternate approach to repelling our mother's attempts to suck us into a blackhole. What if we hadn't argued on the ride back? What if we'd paid more attention when she got uncharacteristically quiet? Maybe we could have sought help sooner or moved with more urgency and care once we realized something was off. Or whatever other hypothetical we could come up with that let us remove blame from the root of the problem and place it squarely on ourselves in a twisted attempt at what we thought was selflessness but was really trauma toxically unfolding the way it always had: convincing the victims that they somehow brought it on themselves.

And that's where the lesson comes in. I remember learning in school that energy can't be created or destroyed; it can only change forms. While there's beauty in the idea of sharing love, positivity, and prosperity with those around us, we can't ignore that trauma behaves in the same way, yearning to thrive, reproduce, and spread as far as it possibly can. That means it's on us, the grief-bearers, to name the hurt, take the time to understand it, confront and address it in meaningful ways (not just slap a quick fix on it), and stay alert for when, not if, it tries to return and wreak havoc. My pain doesn't need to be passed on to my chosen friends and family. And it won't be. Will it spill out sometimes? Of course. But can I recognize it and catch it before it does lasting damage? I'll die trying. Misery may love company, but the property owners get to decide who's welcomed on the premises.

No Strings Attached

I spent over two decades hating my father. Period. Even now, as I share my story, I can sense that I haven't painted him with a redemptive brush. If anything, I may have blurred and compounded memories through a lens of disgusted disdain. When I remember him, I see a man who was supposed to be our protector but instead inflicted harm and left behind lifelong scars, ones that may never fully heal and forever complicate the way I interact with those I hold closest. When I should recall a young boy being led by his ultimate role model, I can't help but feel cheated and angry that I got the proverbial short end of the stick. But once the waves of scorn pass, I'm left with a less obstructed view and more complete picture of the man he was.

Like my mother, my father struggled with demons of his own. And let me be the first to say it- he and my mother shouldn't have gotten involved with one another. Yeah, yeah, yeah, maybe that means I wouldn't have been born. But my existence doesn't change the fact that they were to each other what gasoline is to fire. They only fed the blaze until there was nothing left but smoke and damage. When you take a relationship that volatile with neither person equipped with the emotional intelligence or resources to minimize harm, why would anyone in their right mind expect something good to come of it? Am I saying my father was the victim? No. Absolutely not. Not in a hundred years. But also... maybe?

I don't know if he ever overcame those struggles, but when I visited him shortly before he passed, I recognized that something had shifted. Not necessarily in him, but in me. Maybe I'd grown. Maybe I'd learned to better understand the complicated nature of the world, or maybe I'd finally accepted the imperfections that come baked into all of us. Whatever it was, that visit left me with a sense of closure I never thought possible. It's going to sound cliché, but that was the moment I realized just how important it is to address the issues of your past while you still can.

Sure, I probably would've done a halfway decent job repressing all that pain for another twenty or thirty years but taking the direct route (actually facing it) turned out to be the better one for me. And maybe it will be for you too. Can't know until you try, right? But if not, maybe consider the small steps it might take to start loosening yesterday's grip. Empower yourself to feel what trust might be like again. Consider lowering an emotional wall and letting someone in every now and then. Practice being a little less of a fighter and a little more of a lover with the people who've earned that privilege. Have license to say out loud that you deserve happiness. You deserve peace. You deserve love. You simply *deserve*...

Not Later

I was watching television one morning when I stumbled into a documentary about big cats across the African continent. Menacing, foreboding music played in the background as the narrator set the scene for one of those graphic hunts that always ends with the circle of life playing out in blood-curdling high definition. A pair of younger male lions had just overthrown the old king and were set to take over as the pride's new leaders. "With the most immediate competition out of the way," the narrator explained, "the only remaining task is for the new rulers to kill any cub sired by the recently retired king of the jungle."

Wait, what? Why? I wondered. As if reading my thoughts, the narrator continued, "this is a vital step in the transfer of power. New leaders must eliminate all remnants of the former one to ensure the health and wellness of their own lineage." Damn, that's cold blooded (well, technically warm blooded), but I guess that's the way it goes, huh? Sometimes, for some to continue living, others have to make their exit. Tough pill to swallow, but that's life. As the camera zoomed in for what I assumed would be quick yet brutal kills, something unexpected happened. To my and the narrator's surprise, the new kings showed a rare and bizarre act of mercy, sparing the cubs and allowing them to stay with the group. Perplexed but relieved, I changed the channel. I figured I couldn't end on a higher note and should quit while I was ahead.

Mr. Strader showed me a similar kind of compassion when we met all those years ago. I was sixteen, moody, immature, and predictably self-absorbed. I was more interested in flying solo than learning the rhythm of this random new guy who, if I had to guess, wouldn't be around for long anyway. I'd already made up my mind: we'd be no more than passing characters in each other's stories. But Mr. Strader had other plans. He did the slow, thankless work of earning my trust, drop by drop, until he'd filled several buckets, showing up when I didn't expect him to, extending grace when punishment would have made more sense, offering support when I probably deserved to be left alone, and giving love even when I hadn't yet returned the favor.

God, why didn't I visit him in the hospital earlier in the week? Was I really that busy with work or other priorities? Probably not. But that was the excuse I leaned on to justify my inaction. Or maybe it was procrastination, tangled up with undiagnosed ADHD or anxiety. Yeah, let's go with that. If I try really hard to link my poor prioritizing to mental health, maybe I can soften the guilt while scoring a little sympathy from anyone still reading at this point. Is it working? No? Yeah, not for me either.

Incoming cliché alert: tomorrow isn't promised. I'd said the words a hundred times before, but I didn't really feel them until after Mr. Strader passed. I could've had at least one extra, clear, and coherent day with him if I'd just gone to the hospital the moment Dee got in touch with his nurse, but instead, I let myself believe I had more... time. So, here's another heaping spoonful of unsolicited advice: if there's something you need to say or do (something that's been pulling at your heart) maybe don't wait for tomorrow. Maybe go ahead and say or do it today.

Broken

I love television shows set in workplaces. Police stations, modern offices, grocery stores, restaurants. Whatever it is, I can't get enough. Some of my favorites take place in hospitals. Oh yeah, give me a solid twenty-one-minute episode that mixes humor and heartache with just the right touch of moral dilemma and a dash of that inevitable "will they, won't they" tension between main characters, and I'm locked in.

I remember a particularly moving episode of a show where a young woman came in with heart failure, but the doctors couldn't find a medically relevant reason for her condition. They'd run every test imaginable, drawn so much blood she may as well have been a human sized juice box, and still came up empty. In a last-ditch effort, the lead doctor reinterviewed her, hoping to uncover some clue that they'd originally missed, overlooked, or discredited during the initial intake. Low and behold, they did: her husband had passed away just a few months earlier, and she'd been struggling in the aftermath.

Takotsubo cardiomyopathy. A heart condition triggered by intense emotional or physical stress, causing temporary dysfunction of the heart muscle. Broken heart syndrome. Though the official cause of death for Grandma Nancy was multiple system organ failure due to advanced stage lung cancer, I'm convinced she died from a grief-stricken heart. After losing my father so unexpectedly, she never truly recovered. We spoke on the phone almost every week, and no matter where the conversation started, it always ended with her telling me how deeply depressed she'd become since his passing.

As a parent, who could blame her? I've imagined plenty of tough hypotheticals about my kids' lives: *What if they struggle in school? What if they can't find fulfilling work? What if their partner mistreats them? What if they share a hard truth we aren't ready to hear? What if something tragic happens to Dee or me?* But you want to know the one scenario I absolutely refuse to entertain? *What if I have to bury my kid?* Nope. I don't even want to open that mental door. I'm not superstitious, but I'm not about to put that kind of energy out into the world either.

If I remember anything from my clinical training, I think the concept I'm circling is called a psychosomatic response: when psychological stress, anxiety, or trauma manifests as physical symptoms. The intensity of our emotional states can have unimaginable effects on our bodies. The mind is wild. I once read a case study about someone with dissociative identity disorder (what we used to call "multiple personalities") who could eat peanuts with no problem as "Alex," but broke out in hives as "Sam." Like I said, wild.

So, while time may eventually scab over some wounds, the work of mending the heart and mind must be intentional, layered, and deep. And on that note, I say this with all due respect: take your ass to therapy.

The Little Things

Before Uncle Mike made that final trip back to Chicago, I convinced him to visit his oncologist one more time. I told him I wanted to make sure we had all the information we needed before he left, but that was a lie. A carefully constructed one. I had already purchased a month's worth of morning and evening pill containers, filled them with his medications in the right sequence, written detailed instructions on every bottle, crafted a letter with insights for Ebony, and ensured all his prescriptions would transfer smoothly. By that point, I'd become something of an expert on his condition and treatment plan. I didn't need more information. I needed validation.

During that last week in Minnesota, I was determined to show him I'd been right. I needed him to see that my care, my recommendations, had been the correct ones. If that care was going to be the reason he abandoned everything we'd built here, I wanted reassurance that it wasn't my fault. I crafted my question masterfully: "Dr. Williams, Uncle Mike has a bit of a sweet tooth. He prefers junk food and snacks over more well-balanced meals. As he transitions back to Chicago, what would you advise?"

Gotcha. Dr. Williams was about to affirm everything I'd done and shut down Uncle Mike's nonsense once and for all. I waited, practically holding my breath, ready for the vindication. I could feel the corners of my mouth creeping up in anticipation of my win as the doctor began to speak:

"Well, at this point," he said, "really, anything he eats is okay." Certain he'd misspoken and desperately hoping he didn't mean what I'd just heard, I asked him to repeat himself. He clarified, "Well, your uncle has lost quite a bit of weight over the past year. More than a hundred pounds, actually. He could stand to add high calorie items to his diet to build up the strength and energy needed to fight this disease."

I turned slowly to see Uncle Mike already wearing the smug smile I'd reserved for myself just moments earlier. I was furious. But knowing it was probably unwise to argue with a doctor who had, you know, a couple decades of medical experience under his belt, I tucked my tail and walked away from the appointment, thoroughly defeated. I think Uncle Mike could sense how embarrassed I was, and maybe in a rare moment of grace or humility, decided not to rehash the conversation. He could have. He probably wanted to. But he didn't.

The burden that comes with walking a terminal illness journey alongside someone you love is indescribably heavy. You try your best to offer comfort while clinging to the slimmest optimism that maybe they'll be the one in a million who defies the odds. You know it's unlikely, but the desire doesn't die easily. I picture one of those cartoonish characters frantically running back and forth along a water pipe, patching leaks that spring up every few seconds, just barely stopping one before another bursts.

That's what it feels like. But there's also an honor and privilege in being there for those final days, weeks, and months. If you can stay grounded, you have the chance to help shape the closing chapters. The final paragraph may already be written, but the pages leading up to it are still blank. And that's where the magic can (and should) happen. Tell old stories. Record interviews. Make videos. Or simply sit with them and say "I love you" more times than feels necessary. It doesn't matter what you do. It only matters that you do *something*. And maybe, just maybe, let them eat that candy bar.

Can You Hear Me Now?

Granny struggled with weight, heart issues, and diabetes. My mother and father battled substance use and shared a short-fused temper that matched (im)perfectly. Mr. Strader fought kidney failure for years, relying on dialysis and medications that sometimes caused more harm than the condition itself. Grandma Nancy had ongoing run ins with cancer, having beaten it once before it came back for its final encore. And Uncle Mike's immune system had been compromised since the mid-1990s; a ticking time bomb we all knew could go off at any moment.

But Steven...Dee's dad, my father-in-law, the man my children and I affectionately called Papa, was different. Sure, like most people in their sixties, his body wasn't what it used to be, but as far as we knew, there was no lingering illness or mysterious chronic condition looming in the background. No silent threat. No subtle symptom we could later look back on and think, "If only we'd noticed." Nothing.

Before Papa passed, I had tricked myself into believing in a formula. You know the one: if someone dies, there must have been a clear cause. Old age. A long battle with disease. Years of unhealthy habits catching up. I let myself forget about the kids from my childhood who were taken way too soon, whose lives ended without rhyme or reason. I let the softer, safer version of reality lull me into the belief that if we compassionately move about the land and treat people well, we're somehow entitled to long and happy lives. Papa's sudden and unexpected death shattered that illusion. It forced me to question everything: how we live, when we go, and who or what gets to decide. It took time, but I think I've finally come to understand a few of the lessons life was trying to teach me in the wake of his passing.

First, stop waiting for hardship to make a change. And I don't just mean death. Any hardship. Be honest- have you ever delayed something you knew you needed to do, simply because it didn't feel urgent yet? Have you waited for things to get worse before you acted? Have you ignored that quiet little voice pushing you to choose better today so you don't have to face worse tomorrow? I have. More times than I'd like to admit. I've convinced myself that there would be more time. That "later" was a guaranteed option. That the issue wasn't quite big enough yet.

The day after Papa passed, we gathered at Meemo's house to

comfort one another. By 8:00 a.m., her children, their spouses, and all grandbabies sat in her living room crying, trying to make sense of a world without Steven in it. Our mourning morning became afternoon, which later turned into evening, and at some point, we realized no one had eaten that day. We ordered take-out but only consumed a bite or two before pushing our plates aside. Food didn't taste right. Not without him.

The same thing happened the following weekend. And the one after that. And the one after that. But slowly, food regained its flavor, meals began to feel like meals again, and now, years later, we're still going strong with our Saturday tradition. Every week, all nine of us come together. No one misses it unless a major life event, a scheduling disaster, or an act of Congress gets in the way. It's beautiful. But I can't help but acknowledge the obvious: we could've started this tradition while Papa was still alive.

Like I said earlier, between the ages of twenty-seven and thirty-five, I lived through one catastrophic medical emergency, wrote three obituaries, and eulogized five people I loved. The hits kept coming. Just when we thought we'd found peace, a new war would break out on our spirits and well-being. And someone out there might be saying, "Teron, at least *you* survived. You're here. Isn't that worth something?" Of course. No question. But I also wonder if, for the person dying, the one-time experience of death might be lighter than the weight the living carry in their absence. I don't know if I truly believe that, but thinking it brings me peace. If that means I have to shoulder a little extra, so be it.

After each funeral, once I'd stepped down from the mic and

returned to my seat, I'd sit there agonizing over one question that haunted me again and again. *Why didn't I say that to them while they were still alive?* Maybe that was just anxiety playing its old tricks, but it doesn't make the question any less valid.

And that brings me to the second lesson: why do we wait until someone is gone to tell them how much they meant to us? Is it embarrassment? Emotional vulnerability? Have we been conditioned to see affection as awkward or taboo? Or maybe it's something darker. Maybe we're afraid that praising someone while they're still alive gives them the chance to disappoint us later. Like endorsing a political candidate who turns out to be a disaster and you end up having to issue retractions, walking back your words, and questioning your own judgment. Is that what we're afraid of? Honestly, I don't care anymore. I'm not waiting until someone's gone to celebrate who they are. That's part of why I'm writing this book in the first place: to thank and honor the people who lifted, loved, and stood by me.

Life's too short to treat gratitude like a finite resource. Since Papa's passing, I've made a point to scroll through my contact list to send random messages of appreciation to whoever I land on. I call people just to say they were on my heart. I write random posts on social media, tagging folks who need to hear those words in real time. I'm tired of giving tributes to people who aren't here to receive them. Going forward, I'm putting flowers into folks' hands instead of just on their caskets.

Don't Ignore; Explore

I'm ending this section the way I started it, reflecting on mental health. At the core of it, my challenges have always come down to trauma and identity. By now, I don't need to catch you up on the trauma piece. But I would be remiss if I didn't touch on identity for a moment.

First, I've been engaged in an ongoing, internal tug of war with survivor's guilt. Now, before you start dialing up a wellness check, I'm not saying I wish I were dead. Not even close. But I do find myself wondering why I'm still here. Why I've been granted the right to live and thrive while so many others from backgrounds like mine, some of whom worked harder, were kinder, gave more, and have little to show for it. Some were in the wrong place at the wrong time. Others made the exact same decisions as I had, but fate decided not to be as generous with them. Why them? Why not me?

And what good is wrestling with identity if we don't complicate it further? Take the question of who I'm supposed to be. All my life, I've been bombarded with messages about what it means to be a man, and I still can't make sense of most of them. On one end, there's the traditional image of the "alpha male" (which is ironic, considering "alpha" usually refers to an unfinished product...) who loses to no one, needs no one, fears no one, and certainly shares his inner turmoil with no one. In this version, your children revere you. Your wife submits to you. You size up every man you meet to determine whether you could outmatch him. Winning is everything. You come into this world alone, and you leave it the same way. You're an island.

On the other end, there's a newer model of masculinity that encourages softness. Vulnerability. Emotional fluency. In this world, men cry without shame, scream into pillows to release their rage, and binge rom coms with ice cream and blankets when the world feels too heavy. Your children see you as a dad, but also as a buddy. Your partner is your equal. Competition is fine, but connection is better.

And then there's everything in between.

Layer in my racial identity as a Black man, and things get even more complicated. Now I'm asking, *Am I being too much? Not enough? Too loud? Too soft? Too visible? Not visible enough? Am I threatening to some? Am I palatable to others?* Do I like that people think twice before stepping to me with nonsense because I'm a six-foot, two-inch Black man? Absolutely. Would I prefer to be a five-foot, four-inch white woman when I get pulled over? Without a doubt. It's no wonder code-switching took root in me so deeply: it was survival. I played in one space, operated in another, competed in a third, and tried to find restoration in the cracks between them. People, institutions, and communities say they want authenticity, but very few are prepared to hold space for what it actually demands.

So, what's the fix? Well, it looks different for everyone, but I'll offer this: start with yourself.

Hold on! I'm not saying *you're* the problem. I'm saying the one thing you have full agency over is your own willingness to explore, understand, and heal. For me, that meant admitting I couldn't manage my mental health alone and reaching out to ask for help. And once I did, everything started to come into focus. I stopped pretending. I stopped dimming. I let the real me—the honest, goofy, sincere me—take his place at the front again.

I rediscovered the Teron who didn't need to twist and contort himself to prove his worth to anyone. The Teron who no longer needed to run himself ragged to earn extra points in someone else's eyes. The Teron who could stand firm in his convictions, ready to defend what he loves with full force one minute and then, in the next, frolic through a field of lilies while blasting '90s gangster rap and blowing bubbles.

I'm allowed to be complicated. So are you.

Careers, Commitments, Callings, & Conclusions

Grace Through Soul

CAREERS, COMMITMENTS, CALLINGS, & CONCLUSIONS

A GOOD CHUNK OF my adult life has revolved around, been shaped by, or prominently featured some aspect of work. It feels like just yesterday that I landed my first legitimate job at the on-campus restaurant as a vessel sanitization specialist, with a secondary responsibility in supply chain supervision. At least, those were the dignified titles I came up with since they had a bit more flair than "busboy dishwasher who also restocks the prepackaged items." I fought hard to work my way up the ranks, first getting promoted to run the sandwich bar and grill, and then (much to my dismay) moving on to the cash register. Lord knows I hated operating that evil money box and the horror it embodied. You haven't experienced true embarrassment until you've rung up items totaling $13.56, been handed a crisp twenty-dollar bill, hit all the buttons to process the sale and open the drawer, only to have the customer interject, "Oh, I actually have fifty-six cents! That should help!" "Help? Who? Not me," I muttered to myself, summoning my inner rocket scientist to do the math the register could no longer handle for me.

Failed attempts at elementary mental arithmetic aside, I genuinely enjoyed the work. There was something about people walking in with a need and leaving with it met—all while getting a dose of my classic blend of humor and heartfelt conversation—that ministered to my soul. Within a year, I'd earned the title of student manager, giving me the chance to put my communication skills and growing mastery of the craft to good use as I onboarded and developed each new class of student employees. Though the work was somewhat repetitive and predictable, there was comfort in knowing that each shift carried a degree of certainty in my ability and in the belief that I had enough in the tank not just to survive the day, but to thrive in it.

By senior year, most of that confidence had vanished. While many of our friends spent their final spring break lounging in tropical climates without a care in the world, Dee and I stayed behind as the weight of an uncertain future pressed in on us. Graduation was only six weeks away, and neither of us had so much as a single job prospect. I remember the heavy silence that blanketed us as we sat together on my dorm room couch, holding hands and staring into the distance, tears quietly rolling down our cheeks. I'd never cried in front of a girlfriend (or any friend for that matter), so the depth of vulnerability I reached in that moment was both terrifying and uncomfortably affirming. Despite the fear, I felt certain of one thing: she was the one. I had *believed* it since freshman year, but this moment made it real.

BALANCING ACTS

T HERE WAS NO WAY I could afford a place of my own after graduation, and the idea of Dee and I moving in together before marriage was out of the question, so Reggie and I found a modest apartment that suited our needs amid our humble circumstances. The neighborhood wasn't exactly safe, but I'd experienced worse and wasn't rattled. Where others saw a gas station that attracted folks looking to score drugs, I saw a convenience mart with cheap snacks and affordable fuel. And instead of fretting about the string of overnight car break-ins, I took a more proactive approach, taping a note to my windshield that read, "Doors unlocked. Don't break window. Car empty. Please close door so battery doesn't die. Thanks." Sure enough, I'd often come out to find the glove compartment rifled through and items scattered, but the door was always closed tight and my windows intact, unlike the poor soul parked next to me. Common decency lives, people.

Wait. I completely forgot to tell y'all about the car! That's on me. Uncle Mike gifted me this ruggedly beautiful red and black 1992 convertible that guzzled gas like it was going out of style but gave me the freedom and transportation I needed for job interviews and my eventual campus role in admissions. I loved that car. Built like an armored vehicle with tires that likely hadn't been changed since its birth, I'd cruise through the city with the top down, bumping music as loud as the geriatric speakers could, and laughing to myself every time the muffler let out a backfire to the surprise of dogwalkers and joggers on the street. I didn't care about the disapproving looks or gruff presentation, Bonita Applebottom was a certified baddie and I'll die on that hill. ADHD tangent complete. Now, where were we? Oh, right. Teetering on the edge of a mental breakdown with Dee.

Looking back on that infamous spring break cry, I can't help but reflect on how proximity shapes our perception of problems. The further we get from a moment, the more we can see it for what it really was: a brief season, not a life sentence. At the time, Dee and I were convinced we had wasted our college years, doomed our futures, and let down everyone who believed in us, but now when we think about that day, we mostly laugh and shake our heads. Not because the fear wasn't real or the concerns weren't valid, but because we were too young and too green to know that most things, including fears, failures, theories, identities, and ambitions shift and grow with time.

As I began seeing things with a little more distance and clarity, it became easier to give my elders a bit more grace for the way they taught me to view work. I remember the exasperated sighs and rolled eyes they gave whenever my generation started "whining" (for the fiftieth time that week) about "work-life balance." Back then, I thought they were out of touch but now I see that their weariness came less from a lack of compassion and more from the sheer difference in lived experiences. Just a few decades earlier, they didn't have smartphones tethering them to their inboxes or laptops that followed them home like shadowy reminders of unfinished tasks. When they clocked out, work actually stayed *at work*. Balance wasn't something they had to fight for because it was baked into the rhythm of life: wake up, go to work, come home, be with family, go to bed, repeat.

For us, that rhythm doesn't exist. Between 1999 and 2019, technology evolved so rapidly that it became nearly impossible not to be constantly connected. Having work email on your phone wasn't just an option, it was the norm. Taking your laptop home became second nature. Using vacation time without first emptying your inbox felt irresponsible and dangerous. Responding to messages while on PTO functioned more like survival as we were convinced it would help us "ease back in" once we returned. The irony, of course, is that we never really left in the first place.

Then came the pandemic, blurring the lines even further. With offices closed and homes turned into workspaces, we didn't have much choice but to adapt. And while I appreciated the conveniences (rolling out of bed at 7:30 a.m., grabbing breakfast with Dee and the kids, watching a few sports highlights before getting dressed from the waist-up, and settling into the "office" by 8:00 a.m.), I also started to notice what we were losing. Sure, I could toss a load of laundry into the washer between meetings or avoid the awkward dance of a crowded workplace bathroom, but those perks came at a cost. Signing off several hours after I was scheduled to, skipping lunch breaks to answer chats, ignoring the outdoors altogether; it became way too easy to let work creep into every inch of life and "bring home" all the demands that came with it.

Our brains aren't built to compartmentalize everything. Even if we try to neatly split our days into sleep, work, family, and screen time (yes, that includes hours of doom-scrolling on the toilet), those segments inevitably bleed into one another. So, instead of fighting, I've tried embracing it. I'm learning to accept that the lessons, tensions, and joys of both my personal and professional lives can actually inform and strengthen one another, believing that it doesn't have to be a tug-of-war. Sometimes, the best way to find equilibrium is to stop pretending that everything needs to be perfectly balanced in the first place.

Kinda, But Not Really...

"**G**UYS, WE'RE MORE THAN just coworkers. And this place is more than just a job. We look out for each other. Care for each other. Support each other. We're a family." I still feel those sentiments coursing through my body from time to time as I drift into nostalgic stupors about jobs past. When I was younger, I bought into that line of thinking, holding that it made sense because I was spending more time with my colleagues than with my actual family, and it was comforting to believe the people around me could be counted on. It gave me the illusion of safety and an excuse to poorly prioritize.

But over the years, that idea started to wear thin. I began to see the manipulation behind the message, especially in organizations where the "we're a family" language was used to justify overwork, under-appreciation, or emotional entanglements that blurred professional boundaries. Leaders—often well-intentioned but occasionally opportunistic—leaned into cultural obligation to family and tried to reroute it toward the workplace. For a while, I played along, sometimes even perpetuating the narrative and sentiment to newcomers joining the team. I'm not sure why, where, or when, but I eventually began to question, push back from, and rebel against what I'd come to call "cult-like" indoctrination, which evolved into a more militant phase of my life, one more focused on challenging "the establishment" and defining who I wanted to be and how I wanted to move through the world of work.

Where I landed was somewhere in the middle. I don't believe work is family. Full stop. But that doesn't mean strong, long-lasting, meaningful relationships can't grow from shared experiences on the job. Some of my closest friends today are people I met at the office. Folks from my years in higher education, for example, don't bolt for the hills when I randomly suggest grabbing a bite to eat or moment to catch up. K-Hat, EE, Al, MAN, Pulles, Asp-Man, MP, Blaire, Gates, RDB and quite a few others; y'all kept me sane in a world obsessed with expecting the best results while providing the fewest resources. Hell, a few of us even became parents around the same time, forging bonds over sleepless nights, spit-up-stained shirts, and the calm acceptance that another human would, at some point, defecate in our laps while smiling directly into our eyes.

Some of those people have walked with me through my highest highs and lowest lows. Some have sat with me in silence when words wouldn't do. A handful even risked their reputations, their standing, and their social capital to extend an opportunity, a connection, or a lifeline when they sensed I needed it most. So, no, work is not family. But if you go into it believing that connection, care, and community aren't possible just because someone gets a W2, you might miss out on something powerful. Put differently: our DNA need not be similar in order to matter to one another. Love y'all.

Show Beats Tell

O NE WORK RELATIONSHIP THAT turned into an almost immediate big-brother dynamic developed during my time leading diversity, equity, and inclusion work in the corporate sector. Y'all remember Brother B from earlier? The guy Shara introduced me to at that luncheon—the one where she volun-told me to apply for a role I felt completely unqualified for? Well, he turned out to be more than just a boss or a name on the org chart. He became the big brother I never knew I needed.

Working under Brother B introduced me to something I'd never experienced before: having a Black man as my direct supervisor. And not just any supervisor; Brother B was a senior executive, a full-fledged member of the C-suite. He was one of the highest-level decision-makers in the company, and I had the incredible privilege of learning directly from him while navigating an industry I knew nothing about, all while deepening my own sense of identity and authenticity.

If you recall, just a few years earlier I'd committed to dropping the act. No more diluting myself to make others comfortable or sacrificing my mental health just to seem agreeable or safe. That commitment had taken root so deeply that I'd become a recurring speaker at a few local colleges and universities, sharing my journey toward authenticity. But as I worked through the mentality shift, I began running into a recurring argument, especially from other leaders and scholars of color. Some insisted that code-switching was not only necessary for professional success, but a strategic tool we shouldn't demonize.

They argued that things like ditching slang or swearing in professional settings, or adjusting our language to suit a particular space, weren't about selling out but about survival. I listened, really listened and yet, something about the framing made me uncomfortable. The old me (the one who second-guessed everything, who would shrink back from a challenge) might have stayed quiet. But not the new me. That's not how I roll anymore.

"There's nuance missing," I rebutted. "Reading the room to decipher the type of language needed to advance an argument or understanding what type of handshake might be most welcomed isn't code-switching. That's situational awareness. Code-switching is when you alter fundamental parts of yourself to allow others to feel better, safe, or dominant. It's when you chip away at your identity just to fit in. That's not the same as understanding a context and adjusting your formality."

They leaned in, so I went on. "Let me give you an example. Authentic Teron is competitive. He likes to celebrate wins in a big way. Code-switching Teron might suppress that completely if he thinks someone in power could be turned off by it. Formality-aware Teron would still celebrate, just differently depending on where he is. He might chest bump on the court, joke loudly over a game of spades, give a firm nod in a board meeting, or send a thoughtful email when rolling out a new initiative with the CEO. But it's still him. Still me. I'm just showing up with intention, not hiding who I am."

Before Brother B, this was all theory. Great on paper, but I'd never seen it modeled by someone who actually had real power. What does it look like to walk into a room and be your full self when the stakes are sky-high? How do you lead while holding on to your authenticity, knowing the spotlight is trained on your every move, and waiting to catch the smallest misstep? How do you "keep it real" without playing into the very traps designed to discredit or dismiss you in the first place?

Brother B was that example. He didn't just talk about authenticity, he lived it. He wore cornrows and diamond studs in both ears, moved with a relaxed confidence that was his and his alone, and didn't soften his tone or modulate his cadence just to make people comfortable. He didn't need to. His work spoke for itself. His ideas were just as sharp whether he wore a T-shirt, polo, or full tuxedo with a top hat and monocle. He stayed true to who he was while respecting the basic expectations of professionalism.

Sure, I'm confident there were times when he wanted to shout, "What the hell are you even talking about?" but instead opted for a calmer, "Can you help me understand your thinking?" And yes, I'm certain there were moments when "Hey, dummy, didn't you read the first email?" got replaced with "Per my last message…" But again, that's not code-switching. That's just knowing the game and choosing to play it without losing yourself in the process. Brother B was the blueprint, and I can't thank him enough for showing me the way. Love you, Brother B.

BLOW THE WHISTLE

AFTER OUR WEDDING, DEE joined a rec league for a few years as I happily resumed my post as trophy husband, cheering from the bleachers but with significantly less heckling than before. One night, the guy in charge of assigning officials was at her game and asked if I'd ever considered donning the stripes and learning the craft. Since I, like most humans, enjoy not being screamed at by hundreds of strangers for two hours straight, I politely declined. But he was persistent and unwilling to take no for an answer. He handed me an officiating manual and told me to come back next week with five rules I thought I understood but didn't. Now, I'm competitive by nature, so I saw this as a challenge. I couldn't wait to prove to him that I knew the game better than most and had nothing new to learn thanks to my superior intellect. You probably already see where this is going.

I was hooked. Completely and irrationally hooked. Officiating became an obsession. In those early years, I devoted whole weekends to the court: eight games on Saturday, another six on Sunday, and with each whistle, I got sharper, more confident, and more determined to level up. My goal was to know the rulebook so well that if someone asked me a question, I could tell them exactly which page, paragraph, and line held the answer. Unfortunately, in the pursuit of mastering this new craft, I unintentionally welcomed back an old flame: perfectionism. Just when I thought we'd had a clean break, there it was on my doorstep, all sweet talk and selective memory, reminding me of the good times. And because I'm a sucker for familiarity, I let it back in.

Did you know that in a single basketball game, there are over two hundred play sequences, and within each, anywhere from one to three potential calls or non-calls to be made? That's between two hundred to six hundred judgments over the course of forty minutes all while being on the move, in real time, with everyone watching, knowing full well that at least half the crowd will loudly disagree with whatever you decide. Now add to that a tight game, passionate coaches chirping in your ear, high-stakes moments, and multiple camera angles waiting to capture your smallest mistake. It's no wonder most officials call it quits before their third year.

You might be asking, "Teron, with all that pressure, is officiating really a smart choice for someone who deals with anxiety?" Fair question. But here's the thing: my anxious thoughts only tended to spiral when my mind wasn't preoccupied with something else. Officiating forces me into such intense focus that the noise in my head fades away, at least from tipoff to final buzzer. It's the drive home, the replay sessions, the quiet between games: that's when the self-critique kicks in.

I've spent hours watching game footage, analyzing every movement, critiquing my positioning, and replaying specific sequences in super slow motion. *Did I miss that illegal screen? Was I in the best position to judge that action?* I've never missed a call from my couch, especially when I can pause, rewind, and zoom in, but in the heat of the game? Totally different story. Dee can tell you I've got hard drives full of clipped plays that I revisit (and not always for the healthiest reasons). I'll pretend it's professional development, but most times it's just good old-fashioned tormenting myself over the smallest error.

There is, however, one particular game I joyfully rewatch whenever I'm feeling especially abusive about my performance on the hardwood. In real time, it felt like everything was going wrong: the coaches picked me as the one they'd "chew" that evening, players repeatedly questioned my judgement, and my partners were making calls on plays that were right in front of me. For those not familiar, that's a bit of a red flag because it either means I missed something and needed to be rescued, or my partners misjudged a play they shouldn't have been watching in the first place, but since they didn't trust me, they reached for something when they shouldn't have. Either way, it sucks.

By 9:15 p.m., I was in the car and headed home. Four and a half hours on the road, which meant four and a half hours of ruminating on what went wrong. But once I pulled into the garage, wired and restless, I downloaded the footage and began dissecting every moment. I needed to know if it had been as bad as it felt. And while I found a few calls I would've loved another shot at, most of the game was actually pretty solid.

Later that morning, I reached out to a handful of trusted officiating friends. Each one listened patiently, empathized, and gave me honest feedback. In true Midwestern fashion, they started with compliments: my work ethic, my hustle, my commitment to getting it right. Then came the gentle but clear message: "cut yourself some slack. No game is ever as bad as it feels on the spot. Also, stop acting like you bowled a 130 and are devastated it wasn't a perfect 300." Before we ended our conversations, each of them wished me peace, confidence, and clarity as I finished out the season. That experience reminded me that I'm actually pretty decent at blowing the whistle and that my officiating community is as solid as ever. G-Ray, Ang, Ams, GarMan, CD, Jess, Jack, Apes, MT, Vick, Sullivan, EP, Nicky, KB, Patterson, Vog, JC, Gayle, Kevv, Mr. Robinson, and a whole bunch of others I'm sure I'm forgetting: thank you. I wouldn't be here, and I couldn't do any of this without y'all.

VOCATION

HOP ONLINE AND YOU'LL find no shortage of career paths, side hustles, and volunteer gigs. There's always something to do if you look hard enough or widen your lens just a little. Dee likes to joke that I've never had fewer than three jobs at any given time, and she's not wrong. Between my nine-to-five, officiating, and whatever random commitments I'd taken on without properly accounting for how many hours exist in a day, I was usually involved in more activities than I could handle and would eventually drop enough pins to make spectators wonder about the legitimacy of the juggling certificate I had hanging on the wall.

As I started being more intentional about scaling back and letting go of certain obligations, there were two roles that remained non-negotiable: husband and father. Cue the cheesy, emotional music, right? On a scale of one to ten, that line probably lands somewhere around an eleven, maybe a twelve. The old Teron would've tried to find a cooler way to say it, something that made the sentiment sound more rugged and less sappy, direct-to-tv original movie. But the more authentic version of me embraces the corniness and isn't embarrassed to cringe-inducingly admit that showing up for family is my top priority.

Now, brace yourself as I make a sharp turn into an unsettling recollection with no transitional warning:

On an almost annual basis (and usually when things seemed to be going well in life), my anxious overprotective tendencies made plans to meet up with my feelings of insufficient ability in my subconscious mind's local diner before catching the midnight viewing of a reoccurring dream that reminded me of my unavoidable rendezvous with shortcomings. In the dream, I'd be walking down the street with a loved one. I can't see their face or identify who they are, but it's apparent that my relationship with them is one in which I'm viewed as the protector. As we make our way toward an unspecified location, an enormous and insatiably vicious dog hops over a fence and begins to chase us. Perceiving that the other person can't keep up with my pace, I intentionally slow down and submit myself to be overtaken by the wild beast.

I scream at the other person to keep running and not look back as I accept the inevitability of my demise, resolved to honorably perish knowing I did my job. Right before the animal renders the killing bite, a different yet equally menacing dog can be seen emerging from an alleyway and begins charging toward the person I'd been entrusted to safeguard. The last sight that fills my eyes before everything fades to black is a grizzly personification of how my failure could lead to the catastrophic loss of someone who'd given their trust to me. I awaken drenched in a cold sweat, with a heart-rate that rivals Olympic sprinters and reinvigorated belief that—even in death—I was destined to let down those who depended on me.

Building a life with Dee and the kids has helped rewrite that story as they've helped me begin to shift my focus from "What might I lose?" to "What do I stand to gain?" That kind of re-framing has been key. It's okay to glance back now and then to remind yourself where you've been, but looking too long over your shoulder leaves you with a crick in your neck and makes it a lot harder to perceive the road ahead.

When my kids look at me, they don't understand the ghosts of my past; all they see is the person I am today and who they think I might become tomorrow. When they call me the "best dad ever," I think they mean it (though I suspect there's often an ask hiding behind the compliment). They believe I can do anything, know everything, and be anywhere they need me to be, which used to feel heavy, like a weight I couldn't carry, but now I see it for what it is: proof that I haven't ruined them, that maybe I'm doing alright. I cringe as I write those words, hesitant to accept that I might be getting parenthood right. But it's starting to settle in.

And then there's Dee. Where would I be without her? No, seriously: where? That's not a rhetorical question. Beyond her love, partnership, and steady belief in me, she also manages our finances, tracks our accounts, builds our budget, and oversees everything from retirement plans to the kids' college funds. I joke that if she ever left me, I'd be homeless within a month (two-weeks if she remembers to turn off autopay for upcoming bills...). She's the one person who's provided me the safety to let my guard down and just exist. Loving someone like me (with my insecurities, baggage, and self-imposed hurdles) can't be easy, and if you ask me, I'll tell you flat-out: it probably isn't worth the effort. But Dee? She's never wavered. Even after learning my full story, listening to my late-night confessions, and bearing witness to the vulnerabilities in my armor: she still chooses me. Every day.

Was there a little bait-and-switch during the early days of dating? Of course. I strategically revealed my "crazy" in small, manageable doses to see what she could tolerate, like a human-sized allergy test where I'd scratch her with bits of my personality and wait to see if she broke out in a rash. But even after she saw the full picture, after she'd had plenty of off-ramps and exits, she stayed. Maybe she's just too deep in to turn back now. Maybe she actually sees me as her soulmate and is a willful participant in the never-ending game of propping me up. Honestly, at this point why am I even questioning it? She seems to be in it for the long haul and has continually encouraged me to chase my dreams with the added security that she's not going anywhere, and even better, will be there to catch me *when* I slip. She speaks life into me in ways I'll never be able to repay.

LESSONS LEARNED PART 6

I'VE BEEN CALLED A lot of things over the course of life. Most of the time, they've been compliments like "kind," "silly," "funny," "caring," "optimistic," "empathetic." Every now and then, though, a different set of descriptors sneak in; ones whispered not by others, but by that persistent little voice deep in the back of my mind. Words like "unprepared," "inadequate," or "undeserving." I've been working to quiet that voice, and though it still pops in from time to time, I've learned I get the final say on how it influences me. I may not control when it pipes up, but I *do* control how much power I give it.

In the past, that voice had the strength to paralyze me, emotionally and mentally locking me in place and keeping me from even trying. These days, when it shows up, I put it on the witness stand and mercilessly interrogate it, relentlessly demanding proof at cross-examination. And almost every time, the voice falters under pressure as it mumbles, deflects, and eventually, retreats. But the internal battle isn't the only one I've had to fight. Outwardly, I've had to wrestle with something as simple, yet complicated, as my own name. With one like "Teron," I've grown used to people mispronouncing it, not out of malice, but unfamiliarity. Still, it happens almost daily. Taryn, Tyrone,

Terrance, Terry, Tevon,, and once, Antwon. That last one was impressive in its lazy creativity. I used to let it slide, not wanting to embarrass anyone or seem ungrateful for the attempt, figuring they'd get it eventually. But year after year, the same folks kept mispronouncing it, which was to be expected since I never conjured the backbone to correct them on the spot. My silence gave them no reason to adjust.

I'm not sure why, but I chose to be an active agent in that change narrative while officiating a basketball game one random evening during a tightly contested matchup. I was granting a timeout to a team's head coach, a newcomer to the conference who was meeting me for the first time that night, when she beckoned me over to ask a question. "Ref, what's the...Wait. I'm sorry. I hate calling you that. Can you tell me how to say your name?" Whoa! I'd never had that sort of interaction on the floor and was taken off guard by her effortless show of dignity and humility. "That's very kind of you to ask," I responded before providing her with the correct pronunciation and capping it off with my classic brand of self-deprecating humor: "...but I'm fine with being called 'ref.' Some people say 'Buford,' others choose 'Hey You,' and I don't think I'm even allowed to tell you some of the things they call me at home..." She immediately burst into laughter, eventually needing to wipe a joyful tear from her eye as I asked what question she wanted me to answer. "Well damn, now I don't remember!"

Took me almost forty years to get there, but hey, it's progress.

There *is* one word I'm called so regularly that, though intended to be a compliment, it feels more complicated than one as I've genuinely developed a bit of a love-hate relationship with it. You might think I'm being dramatic, and maybe I am, but hear me out. Have you ever repeated a word so many times that it loses meaning? Try saying "endure" over and over again. After a while, it starts to sound like warm pudding oozing out of your mouth in a bad British accent. "Enduuuuuure." Ok, got that visual burned into your soul? I have a similar reaction to a word that, on the surface, seems harmless. Encouraging, even. But the more I've heard it, the more I've examined its weight. Ready? Here it is: resilient.

According to the definition, resilience is "the ability to successfully adapt to difficult or challenging life experiences, often described as the capacity to 'bounce back' from adversity while maintaining psychological well-being." It's about adjusting, being flexible, and keeping your balance while navigating rough terrain. In theory, that's undoubtedly admirable, but in practice, true resilience doesn't feel great. It's earned, not inherited, demands pain and loss, and requires that you go through the fire, over and over again, and still come out standing. Smiling. Whole. Functional. That's the part people don't talk about. The bruises, exhaustion, and scars you carry long after the storm has passed.

When I was younger, I wore the word like a badge of honor because being called resilient made me feel strong. Like a fighter. A survivor. But now I hear it and silently wonder how much longer I'll have to keep living it or how many more times I'll be expected to bounce back before someone says, "Hey, maybe you shouldn't have to anymore." Yes, I've learned to be strong, but I've also developed an appetite for softness. To dream of a day when I don't have to grit my teeth or gear up for another battle. That day isn't here yet, but I wholeheartedly believe it's coming. I have to. Right?

Wings of a Butterfly

Anyone else get lost in the game of "what-ifs" as often as I do? Before I sought help, those questions used to haunt me at night, lying awake doomsday planning, building contingency after contingency for every possible outcome. These days, I've learned to engage with those hypotheticals from a different place, rooted not in fear or dread, but wonder and gratitude. I no longer obsess over what's gone wrong, opting instead to focus on what's gone right.

My family and I recently took a trip to the zoo, and while there, a bird flying by decided to...drop a package on my brother-in-law. We all laughed—him less than the rest of us—as he stood pondering, "Why me?! Thousands of people are here; why me!?" As a person with less reason to have a crappy (see what I did there?) outlook at that moment, I thought about all the times birds had flown overhead and not engaged in aerial biological warfare throughout his life and how he should feel lucky that it's only happened once. Of course, I didn't say any of that aloud because I'm socially aware enough to know that no one appreciates a philosophy lesson as they wipe feces from their forehead, nose, and upper lip...

I guess that's the gift and curse of constantly rebounding from pain: you're left with the ability to see how it might have turned out worse, finding even the smallest nuggets of fortune that sometime come wrapped in a ball of dung. When you've persevered enough, you start spotting silver linings in storm clouds even though most of us are only a coin flip away from an unbearably bad day, which is sometimes the first domino to fall in a subsequently downtrodden life. I catch myself daydreaming about that a lot, lobbing random hypotheticals into the air and watching where they land. Sometimes I do it aimlessly, but more often than not, it's my way of grappling with the blurry intersection between free will and fate.

What if Granny's death didn't force my mother to move to Minnesota against my strongest objection? What if Uncle Mike decided to stay in the suburbs, granting me the option to remain with him through high school instead of my mother sending for me at the end of my sophomore year? What if I knew my college of choice was a bad financial fit and decided to go elsewhere? What if Mr. Pointe never told me to build my Black network or Dee rejected my online friend request? Life probably looks a bit different, right? Let's kick it up a notch, shall we?

What if I had paid closer attention to my father that day when he taught me how to load a gun, just in case I ever had to use one to protect my family? What if I had done exactly as he showed me? What if I'd slid in the magazine correctly, taken aim while he slept, and pulled the trigger? I would've been keeping a promise, in the most tragic and twisted way, protecting my family just like he told me to. Would the courts have charged me? Would they have called me a threat? A hero? A child too young to understand the consequences of his actions? Would the judge have shown mercy, or would they have used me to make a point? Do they even make orange jumpsuits in size 5T?

Or what about the time I was walking around with that hyper-realistic BB gun? What if the officer who saw it didn't realize it was a toy? What if, instead of calmly removing it from my waistband, he drew his weapon and shouted for me to freeze? Would I have run? Complied? Would I be here now, or would my story have ended with a headline, a protest, a mural, and an airbrushed name on a T-shirt? Would the people who love me have had to wonder who I might have become?

And then there's the story about me and my girlfriend at the shelter. We were home alone, watching a movie that had just enough sexual tension to push curiosity past the line. She was fixated on one of the scenes and asked out loud whether the woman on screen was in pain or enjoying herself. I, being equally intrigued and only slightly more clueless, asked if she wanted to find out. She giggled, "Maybe…" and the moment escalated.

Just as we began to garner the courage (or stupidity) to take things to the next level, my mom kicked the bedroom door open like a one-woman SWAT team. As only a Black mother could, she greeted us with, "I don't know who the hell y'all think y'all are or where the hell y'all think y'all are at, but there ain't gonna be no f***ing here today!" I don't know if I was more upset *with* or embarrassed *by* the way my mom handled that intervention, but I'm certain she's the reason why that girl and I never took our relationship to the next level. We actually broke up a few weeks later as our families were placed in affordable housing in different cities and thought it best to emotionally and geographically move on from one another.

About a year later, I ran into her again on the street. I called out to her, excited to catch up, and she rushed over to hug me so hard I almost blacked out. We exchanged updates and life stories before I noticed the stroller she was gently rocking with one hand. "This is my son, Xavier," she said. "He's three months old." Now, I'm no mathematician—despite having once referred to myself as a "math magician" in younger years—but three months of life plus forty weeks of baking equals...yeah, she probably wasn't as naïve as she let on during our little movie moment. Still, instead of feeling betrayed or angry, I felt thankful. Thankful that my mother's over-the-top entrance saved me from a life I might not have been ready for because, knowing the kind of man I am today, I would have stuck around, raising that child and staying by her side. Not a second thought and no questions asked. But still, *what if?*

That's the strange beauty of life, isn't it? Every "almost" and "could-have-been." Close calls and sharp turns that shape us without even realizing it. We look back and ask ourselves what we would've done differently, how we might have rewritten the story with the knowledge we have now, but the truth is: every mistake, every miracle, every awkward twist and unlikely save has brought us to this moment. This version of ourselves. This seat. This life.

Buck Stops Here

I'd been looking at my situation all wrong. Before putting pen to paper, my reflections and recollections often drummed up feelings of regret, grief, disdain, disappointment, and (un)healthy doses of embarrassment. And while I'm empowered to experience those emotions however they naturally arise, I've done a disservice to myself and those I care about if I can't acknowledge or accept the fact that my battle axe was forged *in* fire, not *despite* it. What does that mean? Are you familiar with the "glass half full or empty" framework? It's a common one, but I don't want to make any assumptions. It essentially suggests that if you fill a glass to its halfway point, there are two ways of looking at it: half empty or half full. The viewpoint you choose suggests which mindset you might most readily adopt: one of growth (half full) or one of deficit (half empty).

The more I reflect, the more I realize my past doesn't dictate my future, but it definitely informs it. I'm not just a collection of all the hard things I've been through, but I'd be foolish to pretend those things didn't shape me. I see it in the little moments, the daily choices, the things that tug at my heart without warning. Like the school's book fair, for instance. Dee had taken the day off to volunteer at the kids' elementary school, and when she came home, told me all the funny little stories you'd expect after spending time with hundreds of sugar-fueled children. One student screamed with joy and scared the teacher. Another flung a booger when he thought no one was looking. Classic kid behavior. We laughed, but I knew the other shoe would drop. There's always one story that lingers.

This time, it was about a student who didn't have any money and was resigned to walking around the fair with empty hands, relegated to the "free zone" while his classmates scooped up books, toys, and fidget trinkets by the armful. Dee's voice got softer as she recounted the look on his face. And just like that, I was transported back to my own childhood, staring over shoulders as other kids showed off their shiny new finds while I walked away with nothing. Had I been in Dee's shoes, I wouldn't have hesitated to give that young person my credit card, encouraged them to buy out the entirety of whatever section they'd like, deliberately defied any school administrator who tried to stop me from crossing an obviously inappropriate line, and later explain to Dee the two-thousand-dollar charge on our account and why I'd been prohibited from all future school events. Past. Meets. Present.

Even with all the hurt they caused, I've started to believe my mother and father were probably doing the best they could with the hands they were dealt. Through the environment they created, I learned how to survive and thrive, fail and try again, hurt and hope, lose and love. In the midst of their trials, they instilled in me everything I needed to know about how I wanted to support and cherish my partner, raise and rear my children, and interact with the world around me. They gave me the skills needed to be quick on my feet and agile enough to adapt as the wind blows. Without them, I'd have no idea how to be resourceful, stretching a dollar into a full meal for those who count on me most. Without them, I never learn how to tap into those pockets of reserved energy after I've already exhausted everything in the tank. And without them, I have and know nothing. Nothing at all. So, without further ado, thank you, Renee and Henry. Mom and dad. Momski and Pops. I literally, figuratively, and positionally wouldn't be here without you. Love y'all.

There are a dozen more stories I could share to drive home the point, but you get it. You've lived some version of this too. Knockdowns don't have to turn into knockouts. Silver linings are real, but they don't erase the storm. Asking for help is a form of strength. Learning how to find an answer is just as valuable as already knowing it. And feeling your feelings, even the messy, overwhelming, unflattering ones, feels good when you find the strength to do so because owning your story, before it owns you, is the ticket to internal peace.

If you ask me, the whole "half empty or half full" argument is reductive at best and doesn't appreciate the complexities this life has to offer. By definition, aren't half full and half empty synonymous? Or, how about this: don't the contents of the glass matter in determining which is better? We're conditioned to gravitate toward the idea that half full is the "right" answer but fail to consider that an empty glass is much more preferred than one filled with poison. Less tongue and cheek, demonizing those for seeing the glass as half-empty denies people the right to feel downtrodden, encouraging them to wear a smile when a frown might be the better and more appropriate fit in the moment. At the end of the day, who cares how the glass is viewed? Hell, I'm just thankful I have one sitting in front of me in the first place.

Father Of The Year (Relatively)

If becoming a husband and father has taught me anything, it's that I know nothing. Well, more accurately, it's shown me that I still have a lot to learn. I've made so many mistakes and misguided decisions that I sometimes wonder if the adults I looked up to as a kid really had it all figured out, or if they too were just making it up as they went. My money's on the latter because, even though the kids can't tell, I'm winging it most of the time. Some days they look at me with wonder and adoration, trying to figure out how Dad always seems to know what they're thinking. More than once, they've asked if I have psychic powers as I effortlessly fix things around the house, offer life-changing advice for their momentous problems, or deliver the punchline to their clever joke before they can. No, DJ, I don't have a magical toolbox; I've watched at least fifty online video tutorials before I start any project, and it only seems fast because you haven't looked up from your tablet in four days. Sorry, Jordyn; that sage advice is really just me throwing spaghetti at the wall and hoping something sticks, offering the most basic guidance based on similar moments I had when I was your age. And kids, I can finally admit I can't read your minds; I just know your plot to get me to use potty humor because I, too, tried the same tricks with the adults in my life, like asking them to spell out I-C-U-P while fighting back a giggle fit.

I'm not ashamed to admit that I love how highly they view me, interpreting it as them recognizing that I'm doing something right (or trying to). When DJ asks if I can lift the refrigerator with one hand to grab the ball with the other, I feel a little flattered. When Jordyn skips over the context and jumps straight into a question because she assumes I already know all the background, my heart warms. But I'm also deeply aware of their need to see my flaws and how I handle them. When I make mistakes, I apologize. And not like the elders of my childhood, who'd skip the actual words and offer peace through food or a passive-aggressive "Are you gonna sit there all day looking mad or are you gonna go outside before I change my mind?" Change your mind? That's your apology? You expect everything to magically be okay after that? Especially when the only reason I'm grounded is because you gave me the wrong instructions and following them led to Granny's good dishes breaking!?

Whoa. Sorry. That one crept up on me out of nowhere. #Therapy.

No, I apologize like an emotionally competent human being from planet Earth. I walk through my version of events, point out where my judgment failed, explain why my reaction was both inaccurate and poorly communicated, promise to do better, and most importantly, I say the words "I'm sorry." Go ahead, try it with me: I'm. Sorry. Again: I'm. Sorry. One more time, for my fellow shattered millennials trying to avoid repeating the missteps of yesteryear: I'm. Sorry.

Doesn't it feel good? Much better than gaslighting your kids (or anyone) into thinking that fault is a flaw only found in people under eighteen. I also try not to do that thing where parents twist their child's feelings into guilt or hyperbolically and egregiously misrepresent the kid's words in an attempt to make them feel like *they're* the ones in the wrong for having emotions. You know what I'm talking about. A kid says, "Dad, you were late picking me up," and Dad fires back with, "Well excuse me for being the worst person in the world. I was only trying to juggle a million things instead of enjoying what little free time I have, all while being your errand boy." Yeah... don't do that. A better response? "Sorry, I got sidetracked. That's my bad." Let's just go with that.

Here's one that might sound a little strange: I'm trying to get DJ and Jordyn to stop craving my approval. To be clear, I want them to understand my expectations, but I draw the line at letting their self-worth hinge on how they think I view them. Way back in Ms. Shethead's seventh-grade history class, I remember her harsh critiques and how she gave me a C+, even though I'd worked hard in all classes and earned straight A's everywhere else. When I went home excited to share my report card, my elders zeroed in on her grading decision and ignored the rest, which sparked my first "when I'm a parent, I'm never gonna..." promise. Most of those can't be kept because we grow to understand that parenting involves hard decisions we don't fully grasp until later, but this one was a slam dunk. Now, when my kids show me something and ask what I think, I immediately return the question: "What do *you* think?" If they're excited and want to celebrate, I match their energy but also encourage them to be proud of themselves. Not because I'm not happy with their accomplishments—I absolutely am—but because I won't always be around to clap the loudest. Long after I've made my way to the upper room, they'll need to know how to value themselves without having to peek inside dear old Dad's urn for inspiration.

And here's a big one: I'm trying to teach them that love doesn't have to hurt. It might confuse you, test your patience, knock you off your feet from time to time, but when love *consistently* causes mental, physical, emotional, psychological, or financial pain, that's not love. It's abuse. And we have to call it what it is and get the hell out. Through endless conversations with my kids, constant self-reflection, and actively doing the work, I'm trying to break the idea that pain and adoration go hand in hand. Some of y'all might be squinting right now, wondering what I mean, so let me give an example from childhood. Anyone else remember being told that, when a little boy teased a little girl on the playground, it meant he liked her? Girls were conditioned to view "love taps," hair-pulling, being pushed off the swing, or bumped to the ground as flattery while the perpetrators had their behaviors written off as "boys being boys." Mix in teenage hormones and underdeveloped frontal lobes, and it's not hard to draw a straight line from those ideas to domestic violence.

Hot take: this is why Dee and I have tried hard to avoid using physical discipline with DJ and Jordyn. We don't want them to think that people who love you are allowed to cause you pain as a form of correction. This isn't a judgment on parents who spank; that's just me wrestling with my own demons and trying not to pass down more trauma than I already have. It's cheesy, but back in the day when I dabbled in poetry, I once borrowed the quote, "No man is worth your tears, and the one who *is* won't make you cry." Does it set up an unrealistic expectation that love will always feel easy? Yep. Does it require nuance? Absolutely. But does it make people stop and think about the toll we endorse harm to take when it's mischaracterized as love? No doubt. I'll take that level of caution seven days a week and twice on Sundays if it saves even one person from a life of suffering. Bonus question: did the line work on the girl I was trying to impress? Nope. But hey, they can't all be winners.

One Team. One Goal.

Mind if I bash a couple commonly held phrases while I've got your attention? Great. Thanks. "Happy wife, happy life." With no due respect, I'm calling BS on that one. My contentment matters just as much as Dee's, and she'd be the first to agree. When we vowed to love, honor, cherish, and respect one another, we did so as a team, bringing with us our own understanding of what those words meant and merging them into something that fulfilled us both. Same goes for joy: it's not Dee's job or mine to make the other happy. It's about sharing our individual cheerfulness with one another, which creates a multiplier effect that trickles down to the kids. Everybody wins. Yes, we're called to help each other up when we're feeling down, but the sole responsibility of creating happiness out of thin air for another person is nothing short of miraculous, and last I checked, none of us could walk on water, so....

Got time for another? How about: "Marriage is fifty/fifty." Nope, don't believe in that either. For us, it's eighty percent of whatever each of us has in the tank. Some days I'll only have seventy while Dee's working with ninety. Other days I'm offering sixty and she's got forty. We give what we can and show grace when the other comes up short. For those wondering why we don't just give the full one hundred; we've agreed to leave room for a little bit of selfishness, what some folks call "me time." That personal space gives us both the opportunity to recharge and recommit to one another, our family, and everything else we carry.

When Dee and I decided to have children, our second big decision was to learn French. Not the full language, just one word: "oui." (Get it? Because it's pronounced "we." Because that's what we'd become... Yeah, sorry. Not my best). We promised that no one (not even the kids) would be able to place a divide between us. We agreed to always check in with one another before making decisions, and even if one of us wasn't totally on board with the outcome, we'd still present it as a united front. No good cop, bad cop. No "wait till your father gets home." No "ask your mother." Instead, we retreat to a private space, wrestle with potential options and outcomes (and sometimes each other) and communicate the final decision *as a team*. Because, even if they don't intend to, permitting anyone to place a wedge between our unity that makes it appear breakable can quickly and devastatingly become the beginning of our ending. I'd sooner sing '80s one-hit-wonders on stage In front of thousands of onlookers as I publicly and uncontrollably wet my pants. Oui oui (…wee wee… like, pee… See, now I think I'm just trying too hard).

Who Do You Think You're Talking To?!

How do I communicate with Dee specifically? Well, that's a whole other set of lessons I've had to learn (and relearn) since the day we said, "I do." About a year into our marriage, she came home from a community event fuming over something that had happened with another volunteer. Being the helpful, former counselor I was, I sat quietly while she vented, then chimed in with a few suggestions on how to verbally obliterate the other person if they crossed the line again. Oddly enough, she walked away from that conversation more upset than when it started. Know what I did wrong? I went straight into fix-it mode when what she really needed was a nodding head and a few supportive interjections like "No she didn't," "Who does she think she is," or "Oh, she's got the wrong one today." Want a little marriage advice? When your partner brings a problem to you, your job is to quickly and accurately figure out what role they want you to play in addressing it. Contrary to popular belief, it's completely fine (and may even be advisable) to ask if they need you to do something, say something, or just listen. Taking that first step, could save you both from unnecessary frustrations, cold shoulders, nights spent sleeping on the couch, and the month-long bout with back pain that follows. Cool? Cool. That'll be three hundred dollars. I accept all major credit cards and insurance. No checks.

That lesson ties into something much bigger. Something that takes some couples decades to figure out: knowing our audience and using terms that resonate with them. In our early years, Dee and I found ourselves bickering over what were, in hindsight, pretty insignificant things. Missed commitments, miscommunication about who was doing what, or unmet needs that we hadn't clearly expressed. We were speaking different languages and neither of us comprehended it in the moment. I've since learned Dee prefers acts of service and words of affirmation while I crave bonding opportunities and physical touch. Her love looks like moving the laundry along, helping the kids with homework, and telling her that I think she's doing a good job. Mine? Chilling together on the sofa, her feet kicked up on my lap, and talking about everything yet absolutely nothing at the same time.

Looking back, most of our petty disagreements came from trying to show love in our own way instead of the other's. Prime example: we used to work out together, but that came to an end because of incompatibility. I'd be prepping to lift some ego-fueled, borderline dangerous weight and needed her to shove me in the chest, call me soft, and slap me on the ass to get me hyped. Instead, she'd whisper, "You got this, babe," which, while sweet, didn't light the fire I needed. Coincidentally, I learned that using *my* motivational tactics on *her* wasn't appreciated either as she overcame the wincing pain of sitting down over the next few days. In my defense, the handprint went away fairly quickly...*ish*.

Yet another "gentle" reminder that failing to communicate expectations can lead to emotional—and sometimes physical—pain.

Everybody Can Get It

Remember when folks started using email for fun? I'm talking about the early 2000s, when it stopped being just a work tool and became a gateway to the world. Man, those were the days. If you had one of those free internet trial discs and a phone line you could tie up for a couple hours, the possibilities were endless. We had access to everything, and more terrifyingly, everything had access to us. On any given day, I'd receive no fewer than three emails from deposed kings asking me to help them reclaim their thrones and all I'd have to do was front them some cash, promising to repay me tenfold. Tempting offer, but I had to pass.

My favorite messages, though, came from friends trying to avoid a grisly demise by roping the rest of us into their cowardice. That's right: chain emails. "Forward this to ten friends in ten minutes or The Cow Face Killer will visit you at 2:00 a.m. and exact his vengeance." Vengeance? On me? I just learned about this guy thirty seconds ago. What could I possibly have done to upset him? If anything, he should be mad at the townspeople who falsely accused him of livestock murder, sentenced him to wear a hollowed-out cow's head while shackled in a pillory, and left him to starve as the crowd hurled shame and produce. That's a cold way to go. Especially since the real killer was the judge who railroaded him at every turn. I'm not *that* gullible, but I still forwarded every single one of those messages. Just in case.

Funnily enough, it's those sorts of memories that make me think about goodwill and how it spreads. Even now, I reflect on the countless moments in life when I've received some type of protection, grace, or mercy, growing tired just thinking about all the instances I could've been in the wrong place at the wrong time but wasn't, because something (or someone) called me away at the last minute. I feel deep gratitude when I remember the elders, teachers, neighbors, and community members who saw me making mistakes, and instead of doling out heavy-handed punishments, gave me a second (or third or fourth) chance to get it right. I get emotional when I think about the people who welcomed me in, took a chance on me, or gave me the benefit of the doubt even when I didn't deserve it. And you know what's wild? The only thing any of them asked in return was that I *not* hoard that generosity for myself.

But how do you extend that same grace to folks who don't seem to be getting it together? What if they've had chance after chance and still keep making the same mistakes? How do you stay patient with someone who seems immune to growth? Is it foolish to keep pouring into what feels like a bottomless pit? How do you value the humanity of someone who, whether intentionally or not, denies your existence, disrespects your truth, and disregards your dignity? It's not unreasonable to think our patience can only stretch so far before it snaps. When do we get to remind folks that for every action, there's an equal and opposite reaction? When does it become socially (and less feloniously) acceptable to introduce foot to ass in the name of Newtonian science? That's what he meant when he theorized every action producing an equal or greater reaction, right? Stomping a clown who let their mouths write checks their fists couldn't cash?

I don't know about you, but for me, those sorts of questions are more than challenging to answer for any one individual and are virtually impossible for entire groups. When I'm caught between the urging of my inner angels to keep spreading goodwill and my desire to write someone off completely, I lean on one of the six agreements I referenced earlier in the book: grace, reminding myself of the mercy I didn't earn, the compassion I didn't request, and the patience I didn't deserve but still received. And I try to channel that same spirit toward others. I won't lie: it's not easy or cheap and takes considerable effort, but when I pull it off, I walk away with a sense of peace and pride, knowing I gave what I could. And when I'm unable to be the "bigger person?" Well, it doesn't hurt to keep a criminal defense attorney on speed dial.

Doubling Down

Neuroscientists use the phrase "fight, flight, freeze, and fawn" to describe how our bodies instinctively respond in moments of fear, stress, or perceived danger. For as long as I can remember, my default has been to fight. I don't mean to take on an aggressive stance and I definitely don't see myself as a tough guy, but when my body senses a threat, its first instinct is to eliminate it. Unfortunately, Dee has seen this firsthand. More than once, she's been on the receiving end of a near catastrophe after startling me, sneaking up behind me, or playfully jumping out when I wasn't expecting it.

I'll never forget one particular moment after we moved in together. Dee yelled from another room that she was heading out to run some errands, and thinking she'd already left, I walked into the living room not expecting to see her again. That's when she popped out of the kitchen with a question...and that was a mistake. My body instantly flipped into survival mode, sanctioning adrenaline to take over, and before consciously registering what was happening, I spun around and threw a lightning-fast jab—the most vicious, stiff punch I had in my holster. Thankfully, I stopped just short of her nose once I realized I wasn't in any real danger. I apologized immediately, earnestly, repeatedly, begging her to forgive me as I attempted to set aside my deepest and greatest fear of being an abusive husband to tend to her needs. Try as I might to forget, it's not lost on me that my saving grace manifested in the form of an arm being an inch too short.

I haven't done all the work necessary to understand exactly why my instinctive reaction is physical, but I suspect it goes way back. Starting around six years old, I began watching horror movies that were wildly inappropriate for someone my age. Killer clowns who preyed on frightened kids. Dream-stalking demons. Evil toys bent on murder. You name it, I probably saw it. Even at that age, I remember judging the victims: *Why run upstairs and hide when you had ample opportunity to get in the car and drive away? You seriously decided to split up the group thinking it'd somehow increase everyone's odds of making it out alive? You managed to incapacitate the villain, but instead of finishing the job, you decided to turn around just long enough to give them the chance to silently get up, disappear into the darkness, and regroup? Why the hell can't you run without falling down every fifth stride?* I became convinced that the only way to survive was to fight. If I was going out, it'd be swinging.

But that was then. This is now. Like most grown folks, I've had to revise a lot of the things I believed when I was younger. As a kid, I thought if I swallowed a seed, a tree would grow in my stomach. I thought the colorful candies I buried would sprout rainbows. I thought chocolate milk came from brown cows. In middle and high school, I believed my classmates were taking mental notes of my outfits and would shame me for repeating one too soon. I thought being liked by a teacher meant I'd become a social pariah. I believed life would magically become easier the moment I turned eighteen. In college, I was convinced that showing affection toward male friends was taboo, that not having my future figured out by age twenty-two meant I'd be a failure, and that once I hit thirty, life would just coast. As a new parent, I believed that if I laid out our reasoning calmly, the kids would nod in agreement. That they'd never cause public embarrassment. That age forty was when all of life's pieces would finally click into place. And now, here I am, staring at my watch, doing the math on how long until retirement, thinking, *Maybe sixty-five is when it'll all make sense.*

Having a belief, then encountering new evidence that challenges or changes it, is completely normal. It's a sign of growth, maturity, rationality, and self-awareness. Updating previously held ideologies when reputable new information is available doesn't make us weak or "flip floppers," but rather strong and courageous life-long learners. The current iteration of me has evolved past the kindergarten version and that growth proves, definitively, that old dogs *can* learn new tricks.

And that applies doubly to narratives we've consumed so often that we believe there's little room for anything to suggest otherwise. Half-truths and whole lies about our worth and personhood, disbelief of the good we've done and impacts we've had, and an inability to accept the love and recognition we've earned. It's never too late to push through those barriers and step into a world where you're welcome to feel valued. Yesterday's beliefs don't have to handcuff us to the past.

To be clear, I still avoid sewer grates because that's where the child-eating clown lives, but I'm also trying to throw fewer reactionary haymakers before assessing the situation. Baby steps.

I Promise...

Excluding funerals, weddings, family reunions, and work trips, I'd never taken what most people consider a real vacation. For me, stepping away from work always needed a justifiable purpose: finishing a task, completing a project, meeting some sort of obligation. I mean, yeah, I took the occasional half-day to let the plumber in, deep clean the kitchen, patch bare spots in the yard, or knock out some other domestic to-do list item that wouldn't fit into a weekend, but that's not "vacation." Even during the holidays, my time off was spent prepping for guests, wrapping gifts, or overthinking the menu for the family meal. I squeezed in a few hours of video games here and there, but even then, I had to skip the bloodier ones because the kids were usually nearby. According to Dee, "small children don't need to see zombies ripping out throats," and I was "going to scar them with all those shootout scenes." She never appreciated the life lessons hidden in those games, like how zombies can't catch you if you make smart decisions and have great cardio, or that peace sometimes requires war, or that a hero's road to justice is often paved in blood. Apparently, none of that was "kid-friendly" or "applicable." What a newb.

For me, paid time off wasn't about rest or leisure. But all of that changed thanks to a grand gesture from Meemo. One Christmas, as we sat around the tree ripping into gifts (and I silently mourned all the time I'd spent wrapping them), Meemo waited for the right moment to deliver the big one. "Alright, kids. Block your calendars and put in those vacation requests: we're going to San Diego for spring break!"

The room erupted. After months of personal and professional challenges, we were desperate for something (anything) that felt like a reset. So, we packed our bags, stepped away from work, and headed west. Meemo had rented an oceanfront property that put the beach right in our front yard and a small amusement park just out back and each day came filled with new adventures, places to explore, sea life to admire, and memories to collect. Most importantly, we were given the directive to just be. Not worry about yesterday. Not obsess over tomorrow. Just exist, fully and presently, in the now. And being the obedient little rule-followers we were, we did exactly that.

On day one, Dee and her brother stumbled upon something we hadn't noticed in the online pictures of the estate: a furnished rooftop lounge overlooking the ocean, complete with grills, games, and a dining area. Dee encouraged me to check it out, but I kept brushing her off, saying I'd go "later." After a few days of being patient, she elevated to demands, forcing me to concede my inexplicable resistance to venturing out and damn-near carrying me up the spiral staircase toward what I was convinced would be nothing special.

And once again, I ask: where would I be without her? As I laid on a beach chair, watching waves crash against the shore in a beautiful, violent rhythm, I started slipping into introspection. *Even with binoculars*, I thought, *I wouldn't be able to see what lies beyond that horizon. Is the water pulling away from the Californian shore the same water someone in Asia will someday encounter? How vast is the world and how narrow is my view of it?*

What I thought would be a quick fifteen-minute daydream turned into a two-hour deep dive into existence, identity, and the sacred act of holding tight to what truly matters while loosening my grip on everything else. I mentally flipped through the pages of my life and paused on one in particular: the moment Dee and I said our vows.

"...to have and to hold... for better or worse... in sickness and in health... to love and to cherish..." When we made those promises to each other, we did so happily. Without a care in the world. We were so high on cloud nine and sleep deprived from sheer excitement the night before that we could've committed to just about anything without giving it a second thought. Endorphins, baby! The secret that no one tells, however, is that those vows aren't written for your best days; they're preemptively there for your worst. It's easy to love and cherish one another when everything's going well, but the trickier part is holding firmly to those promises when the proverbial excrement hits the fan. And now, as I think about the sanctity of devotion, and prepare for whatever new hardships lie ahead, I feel called to share with you a new set of vows I've made. Not to Dee, the kids, or anyone else. To me.

Vow # One: Being

"Being myself" doesn't mean I get to keep my toxic traits just because they're familiar. If I know something about me is harmful but I'm too lazy, scared, selfish, or unmotivated to deal with it, I still need y'all to lovingly grab me by the shoulders, look me in the eye, and shake me like an off-balance washing machine until I snap out of it. That's how you help me help myself and get me closer to truly knowing who I am. And when I know myself better, I can live more honestly and confidently in the skin I'm in.

I've said plenty about code-switching and pretending to be someone I'm not just to make other people comfortable. Here's the truth: anyone from whom I feel the need to hide my true self doesn't actually *love* or *know* me. They may like the persona, but they can't love the real me because they've never met him. In fact, some are probably waiting to pounce on the moment I show even the slightest glimpse of imperfection that confirms their biases and preconceived notions. I could spend twenty years consistently being a "model" citizen, but as soon as I slip or expose a crack in the armor, that person I'd been looking to impress or curry favor with will joyfully bellow "aha! I knew it!" as they delight in my folly. And here's the wildest part. The day I decided to drop the act and show up as myself, there were people who saw me clearly for the first time and had the nerve to call *that* me the imposter. The audacity! Never again. I vow to never wear that mask again.

Vow # Two: Accepting

Maybe it's a fatal flaw in all formerly broken kids who grow into slightly less broken adults, but imposter syndrome is real and tends to prevent me from feeling worthy, accomplished, or as if I belong. Although my friends, family, and community are constantly speaking life into me and celebrating the impact I've had, I'm always ready with a well-rehearsed diminishment or dismantling of their recognition.

Like the time my alma mater informed me I'd been selected for an award given annually to one graduate under the age of forty who exemplifies equity and inclusion. *Of the nearly twenty-thousand eligible alumni, they chose me?* It took Dee and a trusted mentor verbally dragging me off the ledge to convince me not to decline it out of self-doubt. Thank goodness they did; refusing that honor would have been one of the biggest and worst decisions of my life up until that point. When I arrived at the ceremony, I was floored. My face was on every screen and wall, alongside testimonials from community members about my impact. DJ and Jordyn lit up with pride as they watched my tribute video, cheering as I walked across the stage. Yet and still, I couldn't shake the feeling that I didn't belong. Other recipients had done things like build schools in Uganda, teach neuroscience, or treat patients while battling brain cancer. And there I was... just me.

But over the course of the evening, I was reminded, repeatedly and firmly, that comparison is the thief of joy. That the mark I've made matters. That helping students break cycles of poverty, pushing for equitable funding, transforming hiring practices, and building community-centered belonging is no small thing. That pouring into my family, my community, and the people I love is meaningful work. And that I've done all of it while never losing sight of my most sacred calling: being a husband and father. A pretty good one, in fact. Some might even say "excellent." (Dee is "some." "Some" is Dee). It was in that moment I emphatically chose to commit to the second vow: accepting the damn compliments, humbly believing the hype, respectfully receiving the praise, and doing so without using self-deprecating humor as a deflection. Instead of amplifying the minuteness of my impact simply because I haven't yet changed the world, I'll use each experience as evidence of what might lie ahead, all while attempting to grow into the version of Teron my tribe already believes I am.

Vow # Three: Valuing

A four-pound, two-month premature baby with underdeveloped lungs goes home to a volatile environment filled with chaos and booby traps. A little boy watches as the people he loves fall to addiction, violence, and poverty while teachers quietly work behind the scenes to keep him grounded in something more. A teenager balances homelessness, academics, family, and identity while trying to define the man he wants to become. A college student drowns in an inferiority complex he doesn't yet have the language to describe. A young adult terrified of repeating patterns of the past nearly misses the gift of the present. A husband and father, still healing but growing, chooses to serve, love, give, and be better to others but also himself.

And now you're caught up. I'm optimistic my story has more chapters to share at some point, but before I go, I have a few requests. First, would you dare to let yourself be a little hopeful? Can you believe that tomorrow still holds possibilities, even if today is hard? Can you give yourself grace for the stumbles and space to learn from them? Will you remember that offering and asking for help are both courageous acts? That your beginning doesn't have to dictate your end? That you matter, even when the world doesn't say it out loud? As your teammate in this beautifully chaotic game of life, I promise to try to meet those challenges as long as I can look to either side and see you standing shoulder-to-shoulder with me, attempting to do the same. I promise to practice those grounding commitments of courage, trust, grace, growth, listening, and candor in the pursuits ahead of me. I promise to love the parts of me I've been taught to hide. I promise to see the worth inherently and intrinsically imbued in me from the moment I opened my eyes for the first time. I promise...*vow* to realize, pursue, and execute my value and remind you to do the same whenever we next cross paths.

Laying on that rooftop as seagulls flew overhead, waves danced below, and sunrays offered an unsolicited tanning session, I decided right then and there that I couldn't waste that moment of spiritual clarity or let it pass by without acknowledging and accepting the gifts it was trying to leave for me. And like those chain messages from the early 2000s, I won't allow this book to close without forwarding them along to you as well. My ask is that, in doing so, you'll hold me accountable if you see me falling short or remind me to take in a little bit of that grace I so readily dole out to others. Or maybe my wish is that someone might take solace or find normalcy in knowing that they're not the only one who's working through issues or that the illusion of "having it all figured out" is nothing more than a trope played out on the big screen and social media. Or maybe—just maybe—the outcome will be that someone might read this and have the audacity to believe that they matter or find contentment with the person they truly are. Whatever the reason, I'm wishing and sending you all the courage, resolve, and fortitude I can spare in hopes that you might choose to believe and trust *in you.* That you choose to see the upside of your story and find strength in knowing the hardships of this world don't compare to the durability of your spirit. That you boldly, honestly, graciously, and with the utmost ferocity commit to drowning out that voice that whispers sweet nothings of inadequacy and replace it with the promise of more frequently asking: "What If I'm ~~Not~~ Good Enough?"

Love you

If something in these pages moved you and you'd like to engage with Teron—through a keynote, workshop, team experience, classroom conversation, or in any other way—please reach out directly to:

GraceThroughSoul@gmail.com.

You can also explore his work and offerings at www.GraceThroughSoul.com.

GRACE thorough **SOUL**, LLC

Grounded **R**eflections **A**nd **C**entered **E**xperiences through **S**tories **O**f **U**ncovering **L**ife.

Embracing yesterday's <u>lessons</u>.
Unlocking tomorrow's <u>possibilities</u>.

Because your story isn't **a shackle**,
It's **the key.**